A Practitioner's Guide to
THE ALTERNATIVE INVESTMENT MARKET RULES

A Practitioner's Guide to
THE ALTERNATIVE INVESTMENT MARKET RULES

2001 Edition

City & Financial Publishing

City & Financial Publishing
8 Westminster Court
Hipley Street
Old Woking
Surrey GU22 9LG
United Kingdom
Tel: 01483 720707 Fax: 01483 727928
www.cityandfinancial.com

This book has been compiled from the contributions of the authors indicated on the table of contents. The views expressed by such authors do not necessarily reflect the views of their respective firms. Further, since this book is intended as a general guide only, its application to specific situations will depend upon the particular circumstances involved and it should not be relied upon as a substitute for obtaining appropriate professional advice.

The law is stated as at 31 August 2001. Whilst all reasonable care has been taken in the preparation of this book, neither City & Financial Publishing nor any of the authors accepts responsibility for any errors it may contain or for any loss sustained by any person placing reliance on its contents.

All rights reserved. Neither the whole nor any part of this publication may be copied or otherwise reproduced without the prior written permission of City and Financial Publishing.

Throughout this book the male pronoun has been used to cover references to both male and female.

ISBN 1 898830 50 9
© City and Financial Publishing and the named authors.

British Library Cataloguing-in-Publication Data. A catalogue record for this book is available from the British Library.

Printed and bound in Great Britain by Biddles Limited
Guildford and King's Lynn.

BIOGRAPHIES

Simon Brickles was educated at Cambridge University. He practised as a barrister in the field of commercial fraud for several years. Simon joined the London Stock Exchange, which manages AIM, in 1994 and headed up AIM Regulation from the market's launch in 1995. He was appointed Head of AIM in May 2001.

John Bennett is Head of Berwin Leighton Paisner's corporate department and specialises in mergers and acquisitions, corporate finance and private equity transactions. He is named as a leading corporate lawyer in *Chambers Guide to the Legal Profession*.

Nick Williams is a partner with Hammond Suddards Edge, which has one of the largest corporate departments among City law firms and is one of the most active law firms involved with AIM. He has a broad experience of flotations, public and private fundraisings and public and private M&A transactions, particularly those with a cross-border element.

Tom Mackay is Head of the company/commercial department at Amhurst Brown Colombotti (ABC), Solicitors, London. Tom was formerly head of legal department, London Stock Exchange and was also a Director and head of legal department, 3i PLC and is a member of the Law Society's Company Law Committee. Tom specialises in fund raising and financial services.

Jennifer Carter Shaw is a partner at Amhurst Brown Colombotti, a niche West End practice specialising in corporate finance. After spending several years in the City, Jennifer moved to Amhurst Brown Colombotti in 1999. She has expertise in all aspects of equity fundraising as well as in advising high growth companies on a range of commercial matters including protection of intellectual property, contractual issues and share option schemes.

Ann Kennedy is a partner at Deloitte and Touche where she is in charge of corporate finance in the Southern region and heads the Deloitte & Touche Corporate Finance leisure sector team.

Ann has seventeen years' corporate finance experience, including two years at Kleinwort Benson in the mid-eighties. Her experience, gained both within the firm and at Kleinwort Benson, covers a wide range of corporate finance activities including venture capital, public issues, cross-border acquisitions and corporate reconstructions. Ann is authorised by the Stock Exchange to act as nominated adviser or sponsor to companies joining AIM or the Full List.

John Wakefield is a director at Rowan Dartington & Co. Limited. John qualified and practised for five years as a solicitor with McKenna & Co., specialising in company and corporate work. In 1985 he joined stockbrokers Williams de Broe, in London, to help in establishing their newly formed corporate finance department. He joined Rowan Dartington as a director in 1991, participating as a founder shareholder in its subsequent buy-out in 1992 and has considerable experience of sourcing capital for companies and has been involved in over 30 company flotations.

John Jackson is a partner at DLA where he has been based since 1995. In the last 16 years John has been involved in all manner of corporate finance transactions as varied as flotations, take-overs, rights issues, placings, re-organisations, de-mergers, joint ventures as well as general M&A work and MBO/MBIs. He has extensive experience of "take private" transactions. John was formerly a partner at Davies Arnold Cooper and was also a partner at Haycocks & Jackson and is a member of The Law Society.

CONTENTS

Chapter 1
THE ALTERNATIVE INVESTMENT MARKET 1
Simon Brickles
Head of AIM
London Stock Exchange Plc

1.1	Introduction	1
1.2	Who can act as a nominated adviser?	2
1.3	Checking whether companies are appropriate for AIM	3
1.4	Ongoing role of a nominated advisers after admission	3
1.5	A company's prospectus	4
1.6	The AIM Rules	4
1.7	A successful market for smaller, growth companies	4

Chapter 2
THE STATUTORY FRAMEWORK 5
John Bennett
Partner
Berwin Leighton Paisner

2.1	Introduction	5
2.2	Legislation	6
2.2.1	The EC Prospectus Directive	6
2.2.2	The Public Offers of Securities Regulations 1995	6
2.2.3	The Companies Act 1985	7
2.2.4	Investment advertisements	9
2.2.5	Financial promotion	9
2.3	When the POS Regulations apply	10
2.3.1	Is there an "offer" of securities "to the public"?	10
2.3.2	Is the offer made to the public "in the United Kingdom"?	11
2.3.3	Is the offer "the first time" those securities have been offered to the public in the UK?	11
2.3.4	Does an exemption apply?	12
2.4	Publication of the prospectus	13
2.5	Contents of the prospectus	14
2.6	Supplementary prospectuses	15

2.7   Liability 16
2.7.1 Criminal liability 16
2.7.2 Civil liability 16
2.8   The Admission Document 18
2.9   Conclusion 18

Chapter 3
THE AIM RULES: ELIGIBLE COMPANIES, THE ROLE OF THE NOMINATED ADVISER AND THE REGULATORY REGIME 19
Nick Williams
Partner
Hammond Suddards Edge

3.1   Introduction 19
3.2   Eligible companies 22
3.2.1 Basic requirements 23
3.2.2 Suitability for Admission 26
3.2.3 Re-organisation and rationalisation of share structure 27
3.2.4 Additional pre-Admission arrangements 28
3.3   Directors and employees 28
3.3.1 Role of directors 28
3.3.2 Lock-ins (Rule 7) 29
3.3.3 Notifying change in directors (Rule 15) 31
3.3.4 Restrictions on dealings in AIM securities (Rule 19) 31
3.3.5 Directors' responsibilities (Rule 27) 31
3.3.6 Directors' disclosure (Rule 27) 31
3.3.7 Advice from the nominated adviser (Rule 27) 31
3.4   Nominated adviser 32
3.4.1 Role of the nominated adviser 32
3.4.2 Register of nominated advisers (Rule 34) 33
3.4.3 Eligibility criteria – obtaining approval as a
      nominated adviser 33
3.4.4 Eligibility criteria – ongoing obligations of a
      nominated adviser 37
3.4.5 Eligibility criteria – monitoring performance 39
3.4.6 Nominated adviser's agreement 41
3.4.7 Nominated adviser's responsibilities on admission
      of securities (Rule 34) 44

Table of Contents

3.4.8	Nominated adviser's further obligations (Rule 34)	.45
3.5	Publication and disclosure of information	.46
3.5.1	Wide powers to require publication (Rule 20)	.46
3.5.2	The Exchange's power to make disclosure (Rule 21)	.46
3.6	Sanctions	.47
3.6.1	Failure to have a nominated adviser (Rule 30)	.47
3.6.2	Investor protection (Rules 35 and 36)	.48
3.6.3	Disciplinary action against an AIM Company (Rule 37)	.48
3.6.4	Disciplinary action against a nominated adviser (Rule 38)	.48
3.6.5	Disciplinary process (Rule 39)	.49
3.6.6	Appeals (Rule 40)	.49

Chapter 4
THE ADMISSION DOCUMENT AND THE APPLICATION PROCEDURE 51

Tom Mackay
Partner – Head of ABC Corporate
Jennifer Carter Shaw
Partner
Amhurst Brown Colombotti

4.1	Introduction	.51
4.2	The Admission Document	.52
4.3	Preliminary documents	.54
4.3.1	List of documents	.54
4.3.2	List of parties	.54
4.3.3	Timetable	.54
4.3.4	Letters of appointment	.55
4.3.5	Legal questionnaire	.55
4.4	Minutes and internal re-organisation	.55
4.4.1	Share for share exchange	.55
4.4.2	Extraordinary General Meeting ("EGM")	.55
4.4.3	Pathfinder board meeting	.55
4.4.4	AIM board meeting	.56
4.4.5	Issue board meeting	.56
4.5	Public relations	.56
4.6	Placing agreement	.57
4.6.1	Conditionality	.57
4.6.2	Obligations of the broker	.57

4.6.3	Warranties	57
4.6.4	Limits on warranties	57
4.6.5	Time limits on warranties	58
4.6.6	Restrictions on disposals	58
4.7	Verification	58
4.7.1	Verification notes	58
4.7.2	Directors' responsibilities	59
4.7.3	Documentary and third party evidence	59
4.7.4	Confidentiality and scope of verification notes	60
4.8	Financial due diligence	60
4.8.1	Long-form report	60
4.8.2	Board memorandum on financial reporting procedures	60
4.8.3	Working capital memorandum	61
4.8.4	Report on any profit forecast, estimate or projection	61
4.8.5	Indebtedness statement	61
4.8.6	Estimate of expenses of issue	62
4.9	Directors	62
4.9.1	Directors' questionnaires	62
4.9.2	Memorandum on the responsibilities and liabilities of directors	62
4.9.3	Responsibility letter signed by directors	63
4.9.4	Powers of attorney signed by each director	63
4.9.5	Directors' service agreements	63
4.9.6	Share option schemes	63
4.9.7	Dealing code	64
4.10	Tax	64
4.11	Insurance	64
4.12	Application to the Exchange	64
4.12.1	Ten-day information	64
4.12.2	Three-day information	65
4.12.3	Charges	65
4.12.4	Additional documentation	66
4.12.5	Admission	66

Chapter 5
CONTINUING OBLIGATIONS AND TRANSACTIONS 67
Ann Kennedy
Partner
Deloitte & Touche

5.1	Introduction	.67
5.2	Company Announcements Office	.67
5.3	General disclosure obligations	.68
5.3.1	Price-sensitive information	.68
5.3.2	Material change	.69
5.3.3	Substantial share interests	.70
5.3.4	Director's deals	.71
5.3.5	Board changes	.71
5.3.6	Change of nominated adviser or broker	.72
5.3.7	Change in the number of securities in issue	.72
5.3.8	Decision on dividend payment	.72
5.3.9	Other general disclosure obligations	.72
5.4	Financial reporting	.73
5.4.1	Publication of annual accounts	.73
5.4.2	Publication of half-yearly report	.73
5.5	Transactions	.75
5.5.1	Class tests	.75
5.5.2	Substantial transaction	.76
5.5.3	Related party transaction	.76
5.5.4	Reverse takeovers	.77
5.5.5	Aggregation of transactions	.78
5.6	Further share issues	.78
5.7	The City Code on Takeovers and Mergers	.79
5.8	Other eligibility requirements and restrictions	.79
5.8.1	Continuing eligibility	.79
5.8.2	Nominated adviser	.80
5.8.3	Broker	.80
5.8.4	Director's share dealing	.80
5.8.5	Transferability of shares	.81
5.8.6	Securities to be admitted	.81
5.8.7	Fees	.81
5.8.8	Directors responsibility for compliance	.81

Chapter 6
THE TRADING RULES 83
John Wakefield
Director and Head of Corporate Finance
Rowan Dartington & Co Limited

6.1	Introduction	.83
6.2	The SEAT PLUS system	.83
6.3	Information requirements	.84
6.4	The market practitioners	.87
6.4.1	The role of the nominated broker	.88
6.4.2	The role of the market maker	.89
6.5	Liquidity	.91
6.6	The after-market	.92
6.7	Relations with investors	.93
6.8	Reporting and settlement	.94
6.9	Market regulation	.95
6.9.1	Insider dealing	.95
6.9.2	Dealing announcements	.99
6.9.3	Integrated Monitoring and Surveillance System ("IMAS")	.101
6.10	Information about AIM companies	.101

Chapter 7
DIRECTORS' DEALINGS 103
John Jackson
Partner
DLA

7.1	Introduction	.103
7.2	Directors and applicable employees	.103
7.3	Dealings	.104
7.4	Close period	.104
7.5	Unpublished price-sensitive information	.105
7.6	Exemptions from Rule 19	.105
7.7	Notification to the Company Announcements Office	.106
7.8	Dealings by a director's or employees family	.106
7.9	Breach of Rule 19	.106

Table of Contents

Chapter 8
CORPORATE GOVERNANCE 109
John Jackson
Partner
DLA

8.1	Introduction	.109
8.2	What is it and why is it an issue?	.111
8.3	How does it affect AIM companies?	.112
8.4	What are the key issues for public limited company directors?	.112
8.5	Directors' remuneration	.113
8.6	The re-election of directors	.115
8.7	Shareholders	.115
8.8	Conclusion	.116

MODEL DOCUMENTATION 117
Tom Mackay
Partner – Head of ABC Corporate
Amhurst Brown Colombotti

Appendix 1 – Admission Document 119
Appendix 2 – AIM Admission Timetable 179
Appendix 3 – Board Minutes for AIM Application 189
Appendix 4 – Index of Documents for AIM Application 199

CONTACT DIRECTORIES 205

Directory of Nominated Advisers 207
Directory of Companies Trading on AIM .217

INDEX 231

Chapter 1
THE ALTERNATIVE INVESTMENT MARKET

Simon Brickles
Head of AIM
London Stock Exchange Plc

1.1   Introduction

The Alternative Investment Market ("AIM") opened in June 1995. It is the London Stock Exchange plc's ("the Exchange") market for smaller, growing companies. No particular track record is required by companies, there is no minimum size requirement nor any need to have a designated number of shareholders. AIM was designed to be as flexible as possible. It is open to companies from many different from differen sectors and countries across the world.

However, all prospective and existing AIM companies must retain a "nominated adviser". These nominated advisers are responsible for warranting to the Exchange that a company is appropriate for AIM. This is a particularly important task given that the Exchange neither examines the suitability of individual AIM companies nor routinely vets their prospectuses.

The bureaucracy imposed by the Exchange is minimal. In the ordinary course, when a nominated adviser declares to the Exchange that in its opinion a company is appropriate for AIM, that company will be admitted to AIM by the Exchange three days later. During these three days the Exchange will set up all the necessary trading systems and notify various interested internal and external parties (such as market makers and index compilers) about a company's imminent admission.

In effect, the nominated advisers are acting as the principal quality controllers for the market and lending their reputations to the companies for which they act. It will be evident, therefore, that the role of the nominated advisers is crucial to the success of AIM.

1.2 Who can act as a nominated adviser?

Given the importance of the role and the level of trust imparted to nominated advisers, the Exchange is very selective about who it will allow to act in this capacity.

Only those advisers approved by the Exchange and placed on the register may act as nominated advisers. A copy of this register is available on the AIM section of the Exchange's website: www.londonstockexchange.com.

The backgrounds of nominated advisers vary. Some are merchant banks, some are parts of broking entities or accountancy firms, others are corporate finance boutiques. The Exchange welcomes applications from suitable advisers from around the world.

However, to be approved all must meet the Exchange's "eligibility criteria for nominated advisers". These are set out in full on the Exchange's website.

The minimum criteria require that a prospective nominated adviser must have undertaken, as a named principal corporate finance adviser, at least three major transactions on major stock exchanges and retain at least four similarly qualified full-time executives. Most importantly, the adviser must be able to demonstrate that it has a sound reputation for corporate finance.

The nominated advisers have a number of particular responsibilities under the eligibility criteria. Above all, they have a duty to protect the reputation and integrity of the market. In short, this means that in addition to discharging their obligations under any specific Rules, the adviser should use all reasonable endeavours to seek to ensure that the companies for which it acts conduct themselves in ways which befit companies which have their securities traded on a respected public market.

Nominated advisers are subject to regular reviews by the Exchange and those who have failed to act with proper skill and care in warranting that companies are appropriate may be censured or removed from the register.

1.3 Checking whether companies are appropriate for AIM

Given the regulatory and reputational risks which nominated advisers incur, they carefully screen companies before agreeing to act for them.

The nominated advisers will co-ordinate the due diligence necessary for them to attest to the appropriateness of a company for AIM. The Exchange is not involved in this process.

The due diligence covers such issues as the background and qualifications of the company's directors, the company itself and the statements which the directors makes about it.

Financial due diligence will be carried out by suitably qualified accountants and legal due diligence by appropriate lawyers. Should the company operate in a specific sector, such as mining, a specialist report may be commissioned to support the assertions and strategy which the company proposes to include in its prospectus.

The process can be an exhausting one but it is necessary to give the market confidence in the quality of AIM companies and to ensure thereby that funding is available for smaller growth companies.

1.4 Ongoing role of a nominated advisers after admission

After admission, all companies must retain a nominated adviser at all times. This adviser must be available to help and guide its companies on the application of the AIM Rules whenever they need its advice. Likewise, an AIM company must seek advice from its nominated adviser whenever it requires it. Many advisers will charge a fee for this service and it is in the interests of directors and their shareholders to ensure that they are getting value for money by getting the advice they need.

1.5 A company's prospectus

Whether or not a company is raising funds at the time of its admission, it will be required to produce a prospectus. Under the AIM Rules this is referred to as an "admission document" and will contain disclosures about the directors, the company's prospects, its financial position and plans and its working capital position.

The AIM Rules are based on disclosure rather than suitability and any failure to make proper disclosure of material matters is treated with the utmost seriousness by the Exchange.

1.6 The AIM Rules

The AIM Rules were completely revised in February 2001. In particular, they were re-drafted into plain English. All references to UK laws have been removed to help to make the market more welcoming to international companies. Similarly, technical jargon was removed to make the AIM Rules as comprehensible as possible to the ordinary professional reader.

The revised Rules are available on the Exchange's website with hyper-links through to definitions and to guidance notes to assist in the understanding of the Rules in a particular case.

1.7 A successful market for smaller, growth companies

At the time that this Guide goes to publication in July 2001, AIM has nearly 600 companies with a market capitalisation of £16bn. It has raised approximately £7bn for smaller, growth companies.

Updated information on recent and forthcoming admissions, trading statistics, company announcements, nominated advisers, conferences and events is available on the Exchange's website. I would encourage readers to make use of this facility. In addition, the AIM help desk is always available to help with general enquiries about the market (telephone: + 44 207 797 4404).

Finally, I welcome this practitioners' Guide and trust that it will assist in the successful flotations of many more small, growing and diverse companies from around the world. These companies have too often been neglected. AIM offers the best of them a way forward.

Chapter 2
THE STATUTORY FRAMEWORK

John Bennett
Partner
Berwin Leighton Paisner

2.1 Introduction

On 19 June 1995 the EC Prospectus Directive was implemented in the UK by the Public Offers of Securities Regulations 1995 which, with effect from 10 May 1999, were amended by the Public Offers of Securities (Amendment) Regulations 1999 (the "POS Regulations"). *Inter alia*, the POS Regulations created a new prospectus regime for public offers in the UK of unlisted or non-London listed securities of UK and foreign issuers, including securities to be admitted to AIM.

AIM is regulated by the London Stock Exchange plc ("the Exchange") and the rules for companies with a class of securities admitted or seeking admission to AIM is set out in the AIM Rules. Under the AIM Rules, an applicant to AIM must produce an Admission Document which must contain information equivalent to that which would be required by the POS Regulations, whether or not the applicant is making a public offer and would otherwise be required to produce a prospectus under the POS Regulations. Generally, a further Admission Document will not be required for an AIM company seeking admission for securities of a class already admitted to AIM except where the company is required to issue a prospectus under the POS Regulations in connection with a public offer and not less than 10 per cent of the relevant class of securities is being offered.

In parallel with the regime for public offers of unlisted securities laid down by the POS Regulations is the investment advertisements' regime established under the Financial Services Act 1986 (the "FS Act") which regulates almost all forms of offering material in relation to securities, subject to available exemptions. With effect from midnight on 30 November 2001, this regime will be replaced by the financial promotion regime under the Financial Services and Markets Act 2000 (the "FSMA") which seeks to rationalise and modernise the legislative framework currently applying to investment promotions in the UK. In order to avoid regulatory duplication, a POS prospectus (which is regulated by the POS Regulations) is exempt from the existing regime and the new financial promotion restriction. An AIM Admission Document is also exempt under the existing regime and will be exempt under the new regime whether or not it constitutes a POS prospectus. However, a company will generally require the approval of an authorised person for the dissemination of any promotional material which is not a formal prospectus such as a pathfinder prospectus.

2.2   Legislation

2.2.1   The EC Prospectus Directive

The purpose of the EC Prospectus Directive (89/298/EC) was to harmonise European laws on the publication of prospectuses for public offers of securities. The Directive was designed to co-ordinate the requirements for the drawing up, scrutiny and distribution of the prospectus to be published when securities are offered to the public and lays down minimum requirements for the contents of the prospectus.

On 30 May 2001, the Commission of the European Communities published a *Proposal for a Directive of the European Parliament and of the Council on the prospectus to be published when securities are offered to the public or admitted to trading*, with the objective of upgrading the existing Directive so as to improve the framework for investing and raising capital on an EU-wide basis.

2.2.2   The Public Offers of Securities Regulations 1995

The POS Regulations were made under Section 2 of the European Communities Act 1972. This enabled the implementation of the requirements of the EC Prospectus Directive by statutory instrument rather than by primary legislation. The draw-back of this procedure is that the Regulations could do no more than implement the

The Statutory Framework

requirements of the Directive and this explains why certain residual provisions of the Companies Act prospectus regime have been retained (*see* below).

In summary, the POS Regulations:

(a) resulted in an alteration to the requirements for London listed offerings by introducing a requirement for a "prospectus" instead of listing particulars where a UK public offer is to be made in conjunction with the admission of the securities to the Official List of the London Stock Exchange;

(b) created a new prospectus regime for public offers in the UK of securities of UK and foreign issuers where application has not been made for admission of the securities to the Official List of the London Stock Exchange; and

(c) introduced new provisions enabling a UK prospectus to qualify for mutual recognition in other Member States of the European Economic Area ("EEA"), thereby creating an option regime under which issuers could apply to the London Stock Exchange for the pre-vetting of prospectuses for unlisted and non-London listed securities, and replaced the provisions under which "incoming" prospectuses from other EEA countries would qualify for mutual recognition in the UK.

With effect from 10 May 1999, the POS Regulations were amended by the Public Offers of Securities Amendment Regulations 1999. These Regulations made changes to the circumstances in which an offer of securities is deemed not to be an offer to the public for the purposes of the POS Regulations; the contents requirements of a prospectus; the requirement for cross-border offers within the EEA and responsibility for a prospectus.

2.2.3 The Companies Act 1985

Because the POS Regulations were implemented by statutory instrument under the European Communities Act 1972, the old prospectus provisions of the Companies Act 1985 continue to be relevant to offers of unlisted securities by domestic companies. The provisions have been repealed in respect of any public offer of listed securities. The relevant provisions impose substantive requirements on offers of securities. However, the definition of an "offer to the public" or a prospectus "issued generally" for the purpose of these provisions differs from the equivalent definitions in the POS Regulations so that it may be necessary to consider several different tests when preparing for a public offer. On 20 August 1998, HM Treasury issued a consultation paper proposing, *inter alia*, to repeal certain provisions which no longer served a useful purpose. With effect from 10 May 1999 Sections 82 and 83 of the Companies Act 1985 (which concern the timing of the allotment of a company's shares or debentures in pursuance of a prospectus issued generally, and provide that no allotment is to be made unless a minimum subscription is received) were repealed except for the purposes of prospectuses regulated by the POS Regulations.

The residual provisions which still apply to offers by domestic companies of unlisted securities include the following:

(a) Section 81 of the Companies Act 1985 contains a prohibition on private companies offering shares or debentures to the public. Because the definition of "the public" for this purpose differs from the definitions in the POS Regulations, there could be circumstances where a private company could make an offer, which would not be "offered to the public" requiring a prospectus under the POS Regulations, but which would contravene Section 81 of the Companies Act 1985.

(b) Section 82 of the Companies Act 1985 requires that, where a POS Regulations' prospectus has been "issued generally", there is a delay of three days in processing applications or making allotments of securities.

(c) Section 83 provides that no allotment is to be made of any share capital of a company offered to the public for subscription unless a minimum subscription, which must be set out in a POS Regulations' prospectus, is received.

(d) Section 84 provides that no allotment can take place unless the issue is fully subscribed or the offer states that, even if it is not fully subscribed, the actual amount of capital subscribed may be allotted in any event, or in the event of specified conditions being satisfied.

The Statutory Framework

(e) Section 97 of the Companies Act 1985 requires a prospectus to disclose commissions to be paid where a UK company makes an "offer to the public" of unlisted or non-London listed shares. Because of the discrepancy between the definitions of "public offer" for this purpose and as used in the POS Regulations, there may continue to be a residual category of offers which are not regulated by the POS Regulations to which Section 97 would continue to apply.

2.2.4 *Investment advertisements*

Section 57 of the FS Act, which will be replaced by the new financial promotion regime (*see* below) from midnight on 30 November 2001, prohibits the issue of an investment advertisement unless it is issued or approved by a person authorised under the Financial Services Authority to carry on investment business, or an exemption applies. An "investment advertisement" is widely defined and includes almost all publications in relation to offerings of securities.

There are exemptions for a POS prospectus and any related advertisement which contains no information other than certain prescribed information. A "quasi-POS prospectus", such as an Admission Document, which is drawn up to the standard of a POS prospectus but where no POS prospectus is actually required because there is no offer to the public, is also exempt.

Broadly speaking, a company will generally require the approval of an authorised person for the dissemination of any offer document and/or other advertisement (and that authorised person will also have to comply with the rule book of its own regulator as regards the form and content of any investment advertisements issued or approved by it).

2.2.5 *Financial promotion*

The new financial promotion regime introduced by the FSMA will come into force at midnight on 30 November 2001. The new regime maintains the distinction between authorised and unauthorised persons and the criminal offence of unauthorised persons promoting investments without the approval of an authorised person, in the absence of an exemption. It renders unenforceable contracts entered into as a result of unapproved promotions. In contrast to the current framework, all boundaries of the financial promotion regime will be set by the Treasury. The Financial Services Authority will then make rules governing approval of promotions by an authorised person.

The new regime broadly maps the scope of the existing restrictions on financial promotion although there are some notable changes, in particular:

(a) the new regime seeks to adopt a media-neutral concept of communication of an invitation or inducement and introduces the concept of "real" and "non-real" time communications to distinguish the immediacy of particular promotions. It also provides an exemption for "conduits", which could include an internet service provider, who have no control over content of a communication;

(b) the framework has been changed to reduce the cost of informal capital raising. A number of exemptions from the restriction on financial promotion have been introduced for promotions to high net worth individuals and to sophisticated investors; and

(c) under the new regime the exemptions can be used in combination.

2.3   When the POS Regulations apply

2.3.1   Is there an "offer" of securities "to the public"?

When a company applies for Admission to AIM, it is important to determine whether the transaction involves an offer of securities to the public. If it does, the POS Regulations apply, whether or not the securities are of a class already admitted. If the transaction does not involve an offer to the public, the POS Regulations will not apply but the company is obliged under the AIM Rules to publish a document containing the information required by the POS Regulations (including information that would be required to be published in a supplementary prospectus) unless the securities are of a class already admitted. Accordingly, in the case of an application for Admission by way of introduction or a placing with institutional

The Statutory Framework

investors which does not involve a public offer requiring a prospectus to be published, the provisions dealing with liability for a prospectus and registration of a prospectus (by way of example) will not apply.

The definition of an "offer" covers both written and oral offers and extends to any offer, or any invitation to make an offer, which if accepted, would give rise to a contract for the issue or sale of securities. Accordingly, warm-up advertising and pre-advertising marketing activities would not normally involve an offer to the public (but they may be subject to the cold calling and the investment advertisements' regime (or, the financial promotion regime under the FSMA) and the advertising restrictions imposed by Regulation 12 of the POS Regulations).

The expression "offer to the public" includes an offer "to any section of the public whether selected as members or debenture holders of a body corporate, or as clients of the person making the offer, or in any other manner". Accordingly, many selective offers (such as rights issues to existing shareholders) will in the absence of any relevant exemption be treated as offers to the public. It will be a question of fact in each case whether a given offer is made "to the public" or "to any section of the public".

2.3.2   *Is the offer made to the public "in the United Kingdom"?*

The POS Regulations make it clear that a prospectus is only required to be published where the offer is made to the public "in the United Kingdom". Accordingly, offers to persons outside the UK are disregarded in determining whether or not UK prospectus requirements apply. Additionally, in applying the exemptions, only offers to persons in the UK need to be taken into account so that where, say, an offer made only to professional investors in the UK is combined with an offer to the public outside the UK, a UK prospectus is not required.

2.3.3   *Is the offer "the first time" those securities have been offered to the public in the UK?*

An offeror is only required to publish a prospectus if the offer is "the first time" that the securities in question have been offered to the public in the UK. Accordingly, if a company has issued its securities in a public offering and published a prospectus under the POS Regulations, a holder of those securities can re-offer those securities for sale to the public without having to register a new prospectus under the POS Regulations.

However, if the particular securities have not been the subject of a previous UK public offer (e.g. if they were initially offered only to sophisticated investors or to less than 50 investors in the UK), investors generally will be subject to the POS Regulations to the extent that they engage in a secondary market transaction which amounts to an offer to the public in the UK.

It seems that a prospectus will still be required if the particular securities offered to the public have not been the subject of a previous UK public offer, even if other securities of the same class have previously been offered to the public. For example, if a founder shareholder retains his shares at the time of an initial public offering and then offers those shares to the public, a prospectus will be required for the second transaction.

2.3.4 Does an exemption apply?

The wide definition of an offer to the public must be read alongside the wide range of exemptions from publishing a prospectus. In applying these exemptions, only the UK element of the offer in question needs to be taken into account. The exemptions include:

(a) a "professionals" exemption which applies to an offer to persons in the context of their trades, professions or occupations, such as pension funds and investment managers;

(b) a "restricted circle" exemption which applies to an offer to a restricted circle of persons reasonably believed to be sufficiently knowledgeable to understand the risks involved;

(c) a "50 offerees" exemption which applies to offers to no more than 50 persons (and for this purpose, offers made to several persons jointly, such as trustees of a trust or members of a partnership in their capacity as such, will be treated as offers to a single person);

(d) an exemption for offers made in connection with a bona fide intention to enter into an underwriting agreement;

The Statutory Framework

(e) an exemption for offers in connection with a takeover offer;

(f) an exemption for employee offers by employee trusts as well as the employer;

(g) an exemption for bonus issues of shares to existing holders;

(h) an exemption for Euro-securities' offerings unless the securities offered are the subject of an advertising campaign that is likely to come to the attention of inexperienced investors;

(i) an exemption for an offer of securities by a private company in accordance with the pre-emption requirements in the company's Articles of Association or an agreement between holders of securities in the company.

Most (but not all) of the exemptions may be relied on "in combination". This means, for example, that a limited offer to 50 private individuals can be combined with extensive "professionals only" marketing without the requirement for a prospectus. However, in order to prevent abuse, a provision allows for certain offers made during a 12 month period to be aggregated for the purpose of applying the exemptions. This would preclude a company from arranging a series of offers to 50 or fewer persons without complying with the POS Regulations.

2.4 Publication of the prospectus

Where unlisted or non-London listed securities are offered to the public in the UK for the first time (and no exemption applies), the offeror must publish a prospectus by making it available to the public, free of charge, at an address within the UK while the offer remains open (Regulation 4(1)). In addition, any advertisements, notices, posters or documents announcing the offer which are issued to the public in the UK must state that a prospectus has been or will be published and must give an address in the UK from which the prospectus can be obtained (Regulation 12).

A copy of the prospectus must be filed with the Registrar of Companies before publication (Regulation 4(2)).

Where an Admission Document for a non-public offer is published, the requirements relating to publication of prospectuses do not apply. But, under the AIM Rules, the Admission Document must be published by making copies available free of charge to the public for not less than one month from the date of Admission at an address in the UK specified in the document.

2.5 Contents of the prospectus

Whether or not an issuer seeking Admission is making an offer of securities to the public which would require a prospectus to be published under the POS Regulations, the issuer must publish a document containing the information required by the POS Regulations.

In addition, an Admission Document must include certain additional information including a working capital statement, a statement of principal assumptions in relation to any profit forecast, estimate or projection, a standard risk statement regarding AIM, a statement of compulsory 12 month lock-ins for directors and certain employees and details of the directors' business interests.

The specific contents requirements under the POS Regulations are similar to the detailed requirements prescribed for listed companies. However, there is no requirement for a statement of indebtedness, summary of material contacts, documents on display, summary of Articles of Association or history of share capital. In practice, an Admission Document will include some, if not all, of this information.

As with the regime for listed securities, there is a general duty of disclosure requiring the inclusion in the prospectus of all such information as investors would reasonably require and reasonably expect to find there for the purpose of making an informed assessment of the issuer's assets and liabilities, financial position, profits, losses and prospects and the rights attaching to the securities. Matters not included in the specific contents requirements contained in the POS Regulations may nevertheless be required to be included in the prospectus under the general duty of disclosure.

The Statutory Framework

The POS Regulations provide for the omission of information in certain circumstances. Information which is contrary to the public interest may be omitted on special application to the Treasury. In addition, where the offeror is not also the issuer, information may be omitted about the issuer which is "not available" to the offeror. There is, however, a requirement on the offeror to make "reasonable efforts" to obtain the information.

The offeror may also apply to the Exchange for permission to omit information which is of minor importance, or seriously detrimental to the issuer, provided that, in the latter case, the omission is not likely to mislead investors.

Information which is "inappropriate" to the issuer's sphere of activity or to its legal form, or to the securities to which the prospectus relates can be omitted if there is no equivalent information.

The POS Regulations also permit specific exemption which apply where shares are or have been admitted to dealings on an "approved exchange", (including AIM). Derogation from the normal requirements may be permitted where shares are offered to existing shareholders on a pre-emptive basis and where the shares offered amount to less than 10 per cent by number or value of shares of the same class already admitted to dealings on the approved exchange. Accordingly, an AIM company may omit specified information from any Admission Document where further AIM securities are offered on a pre-emptive basis to some or all of the existing holders of such securities and an AIM company is exempted from preparing a further Admission Document which would otherwise be required where less than 10 per cent of a class of AIM securities are being offered. There is general power vested in the Exchange to authorise omission of information from an Admission Document in the same circumstances as information may be omitted from a prospectus under the POS Regulations.

2.6 Supplementary prospectuses

If, while a public offer is outstanding, there is a significant change to information contained in the prospectus, a significant new matter arises which would have been required to be included if it had arisen when the original prospectus was prepared, or there is a significant inaccuracy in the prospectus, then the offeror is required to publish a supplementary prospectus and to file a copy with the Registrar of Companies. The provisions relating to liability for prospectuses under the POS Regulations also apply in similar terms to supplementary prospectuses. If an Admission Document is published in circumstances in which the offer is not treated as made to the public (e.g. because one of the exemptions applies), there is a requirement in the AIM Rules to publish a document containing the information that would be required to be published in a supplementary prospectus.

2.7   Liability

2.7.1   Criminal liability

There is no specific criminal liability for prospectuses. However, Section 47(1) of the FS Act imposes criminal liability on any person who makes a statement, promise or forecast which he knows to be misleading, false or deceptive, or dishonestly conceals any material facts for the purpose of inducing (or is reckless as to whether it may induce) another person to enter into or offer to enter into, a contract for the subscription or purchase of an investment. The new offence of market abuse created by the FSMA may also be applicable with effect from midnight on 30 November 2001.

2.7.2   Civil liability

Under the POS Regulations, the "persons responsible" for a prospectus or supplementary prospectus are liable to pay compensation to any person who acquires securities to which the prospectus or supplementary prospectus relates and who suffers loss as a result of an untrue or misleading statement or the omission of any matters required to be included by the POS Regulations. It does not appear that the person claiming loss needs to establish reliance on the untrue or misleading statement.

The persons responsible for a POS prospectus are:

(a) the issuer;

(b) where the issuer is a body corporate, its directors and anyone who has agreed to be named in the prospectus as a director or as someone who has agreed to become a director;

(c) anyone who accepts, and is stated in the prospectus as accepting, responsibility for all or part of the prospectus;

(d) the offeror (where separate from the issuer) and its directors;

(e) anyone else who has authorised the contents of the prospectus.

Where the issuer is responsible for the prospectus, the prospectus was drawn up primarily by the issuer and the offeror is making the offer of securities in association with the issuer, the offeror is not responsible for the prospectus.

Where the directors of the issuer are responsible for the prospectus, they are required to make the declaration of responsibility for the contents of the prospectus. The directors of the offeror will be required to make a declaration of responsibility where the offeror is not the issuer.

The person responsible may escape liability if he can show that, when the prospectus was delivered for registration, he reasonably believed, having made such enquiries (if any) as were reasonable, that the statement in question was true and not misleading, or that the omission which caused the loss was properly omitted and:

(a) that he continued in that belief until the time the securities were acquired; or

(b) that they were acquired before it was reasonably practicable to bring a correction to the attention of potential investors; or

(c) that before the securities were acquired he had taken all such steps as it was reasonable for him to have taken to ensure that a correction would be brought to the attention of potential investors; or

(d) that the securities were acquired after such a lapse of time that he ought reasonably to be excused and, if the securities are being dealt in on an approved exchange, he continued in that believe until after the commencement of dealings in the securities on that exchange.

2.8 The Admission Document

In view of the extensive range of exemptions, the Admission Document is rarely a POS prospectus. In these circumstances the Admission Document constitutes an investment advertisement (or financial promotion after 30 November 2001) which, subject to the exemptions under the investment advertisements (or financial promotion) regime, must be issued or approved by an authorised person. The authorised person, in issuing or approving the document, must comply with the rules of its regulatory body, in other words, the Financial Services Authority. These rules require an authorised person to apply appropriate expertise and to be able to show that it believes on reasonable grounds that the advertisement is fair and not misleading.

However, an Admission Document is exempt from the investment advertisements regime and will be exempt from the financial promotion regime. Its contents are governed by the AIM Rules which form the basis of a contract between the Exchange and the issuer.

Criminal sanctions may arise from false or misleading statements in the Admission Document. In addition, directors and others who authorise the issue of the Admission Document are potentially liable at common law for any fraudulent or negligent mis-statements made in the document.

2.9 Conclusion

AIM has been in operation under the current statutory framework for six years. In May 1999, the POS Regulations were amended and a number of the exemptions from the obligation to produce a prospectus were expanded modestly by making more effective use of the exemptions permitted under the EC Prospectus Directive. The main piece of unfinished business is that the Treasury is proposing to amend the residual prospectus provisions contained in the Companies Act 1985 so as to remove, wherever possible, any inconsistencies with the POS Regulations.

Chapter 3

THE AIM RULES: ELIGIBLE COMPANIES, THE ROLE OF THE NOMINATED ADVISER AND THE REGULATORY REGIME

Nick Williams
Partner
Hammond Suddards Edge

3.1 Introduction

The Rules applying to companies wishing to obtain and maintain a listing for their shares on AIM ("the AIM Rules") are published by the London Stock Exchange plc ("the Exchange"). Reflecting the results of wide-spread consultation prior to AIM's launch about the needs of growing companies, the Exchange has set accessible entry requirements and relatively relaxed continuing obligations. This is evidenced by the brevity of the AIM Rules, as compared to the Listing Rules for companies listed (or applying to be listed) on the Official List.

Also relevant is Chapter 17 of the Rules of the Exchange, which regulates trading in AIM shares. The current version of the AIM Rules and other relevant information are available on the Exchange's website at www.londonstockexchange.com.

The relatively relaxed regulatory regime is made possible by the requirement that each company applying and admitted to AIM appoints a nominated adviser, which is a professional firm complying with the eligibility criteria published by the Exchange and responsible to it. It is the obligation of the nominated adviser to take appropriate steps with a view to ensuring that the directors of a company applying for the first time to have a class of its securities admitted to AIM (" Applicant Co") or of a company with a class of its securities admitted to AIM ("AIM Company") are aware of their responsibilities and obligations under the AIM Rules and that each such company complies with such Rules. In turn, the directors are required to seek advice and guidance from the nominated adviser and to take it into account. The nominated adviser is also required to confirm to the Exchange that it considers an Applicant Co and its securities to be "appropriate" for admission when that Applicant Co and its securities are first admitted to trading on AIM ("Admission"). The Exchange has the power to impose sanctions on the company and the nominated adviser.

The AIM Rules were revised with effect from February 2001 and comprise the following:

(a) *Eligibility for AIM (Rule 1)*: the requirement for an Applicant Co to appoint a nominated adviser;

(b) *Applicants for AIM (Rules 2 to 6)*: a description of the information and documents, including the principal document published at the time of Admission ("the Admission Document"), which must be provided to the Exchange prior to Admission, and an explanation of when Admission becomes effective;

(c) *Special conditions for certain Applicant Cos (Rules 7 and 8)*: a requirement for the related parties and applicable employees as at the date of Admission of an Applicant Co whose main activity is a business which has not been independent and earning revenue for at least two years to retain any of that company's AIM securities they hold for one year from Admission and provision for the Exchange to make Admission subject to a special condition and to delay Admission in certain circumstances;

(d) *Principles of disclosure (Rule 9)*: the procedures for notifying information to the Company Announcements Office ("CAO");

(e) *General disclosure of price sensitive information (Rule 10)*: a requirement for an AIM Company to notify price sensitive information (information which, if made public, would be likely to lead to a substantial movement in the price of its AIM securities) to the CAO;

The AIM Rules

(f) *Disclosure of corporate transactions (Rules 11 to 14)*: a description of the requirements for disclosure and approval of significant and related party transactions;

(g) *Disclosure of miscellaneous information (Rule 15)*: matters that must be notified to the CAO without delay;

(h) *Half yearly reports (Rule 16)*: an AIM Company has to prepare half-yearly financial reports;

(i) *Annual accounts (Rule 17)*: the requirements for audited annual accounts of AIM Companies;

(j) *Publication of documents sent to shareholders (Rule 18)*: rules for publication and availability of documents provided to holders of AIM securities;

(k) *Restrictions on deals (Rule 19)*: restrictions on dealing by directors and applicable employees in AIM securities;

(l) *Provision and disclosure of information (Rules 20 and 21)*: the ability of the Exchange to require or disclose information;

(m) *Further issues of securities following Admission (Rules 22 to 25)*: requirements where further securities are issued by an AIM Company following its Admission;

(n) *Language (Rule 26): all relevant documents to be in English*;

(o) *Directors' responsibility for compliance (Rule 27)*: the directors of an AIM Company are responsible for compliance with the AIM Rules, for disclosing relevant information and seeking advice from the nominated adviser;

(p) *Ongoing eligibility requirements (Rules 28 to 33)*: requirements to be met by an AIM Company on and following Admission;

(q) *Nominated advisers (Rule 34)*: responsibilities of nominated advisers;

(r) *Maintenance of orderly markets (Rules 35 and 36)*: circumstances in which the Exchange may suspend trading or cancel the admission of AIM securities;

A Practitioner's Guide to the Alternative Investment Market Rules

(s) *Sanctions and appeals (Rules 37 to 40)*: disciplinary action the Exchange may take against an AIM Company or a nominated adviser;

(t) *Schedule One*: information which an Applicant Co must provide to the Exchange pursuant to Rule 2;

(u) *Schedule Two*: information that must be disclosed in an Admission Document;

(v) *Schedule Three*: the "class tests" for determining the size of a transaction pursuant to Rules 11, 12, 13 and 17;

(w) *Schedule Four*: information which must be notified to the CAO pursuant to Rules 11, 12 and 13;

(x) *Schedule Five*: information which must be notified to the CAO pursuant to Rule 15;

(y) *Schedule Six*: confirmations required from a nominated adviser pursuant to Rule 34; and

(z) *Glossary*: meanings of terms used in the AIM Rules.

Guidance Notes are also published by the Exchange, which do not form part of the Rules, but are intended to assist in their interpretation.

Where an AIM Company has concerns about the interpretation of the Rules, it should consult its nominated adviser.

The term "AIM securities", as used in the AIM Rules, encompasses the different types and classes of shares and other securities which are admitted to trading on AIM.

3.2 Eligible companies

In contrast to the Official List's requirements (with certain exceptions) for a company to have a three-year trading record, a minimum market capitalisation of £700,000 and 25 per cent of its shares publicly held, AIM's Admission requirements permit young and growing companies from around the world with limited or no

The AIM Rules

trading records to join the market. A further difference is that the Exchange is not involved in considering whether a company is suitable for admission to AIM: as described in section 3.2.2 below, this responsibility is placed on the nominated adviser.

3.2.1 Basic requirements

The basic requirements for eligibility, which must be satisfied on Admission and at all times thereafter, are as follows:

(a) *Nominated adviser (Rules 1 and 30)*: an applicant for admission to AIM and an AIM Company must have a nominated adviser at all times. It is the obligation of the nominated adviser, which must have been approved by the Exchange and included in its register of nominated advisers, to take appropriate steps so that the directors of an Applicant Co or AIM Company are aware of their responsibilities and obligations to ensure compliance by the company with the Rules (*see* sections 3.4.7 and 3.4.8 below). If an AIM Company ceases to have a nominated adviser, the Exchange will suspend trading in its AIM securities. If within one month the AIM Company has failed to appoint a replacement nominated adviser, the admission of its AIM securities will be cancelled.

(b) *Published accounts (Rule 17)*: an AIM Company must publish annual audited accounts prepared in accordance with UK or US generally accepted accounting practice or International Accounting Standards.

(c) *Securities freely transferable (Rule 28)*: securities admitted to trading on AIM must be free from restrictions on transferability. It is suggested that the constitutional documents of a company should not provide for any minimum or maximum holdings of shares or restrict shareholders to, say, nationals of the country of incorporation.

However, there are limited exceptions to this requirement for free transferability:

   (i) where, in any jurisdiction in which the AIM Company operates, statute or regulations place restrictions upon transferability; or

(ii) where the AIM Company is seeking to ensure that it does not become subject to statute or regulation if it has a particular number of shareholders domiciled in a particular country.

(d) *Securities to be admitted to trading (Rule 29)*: a company must ensure that application is made to admit all securities of the same class to trading on AIM. Only securities which have been unconditionally allotted can be admitted. In fact securities are usually allotted in advance "subject to admission". The Exchange has stated that all types and classes of securities, including ordinary shares, preference shares and debt securities can be admitted to AIM.

(e) *Nominated broker (Rule 31)*: an AIM Company must retain a nominated broker at all times and its nominated adviser may assume this role as well. The nominated broker's role is to support trading in the company's AIM securities and Rule 17.4 of the AIM Trading Rules (in Chapter 17 of the Rules of the Exchange) provides that the nominated broker during a mandatory quote period (as at July 2001 the period between 8.00 am and 4.30 pm on each day on which the Exchange is open) must, if requested, use its best endeavours to match buy and sell orders in those AIM securities if there is no registered market maker in the securities. A market maker is an Exchange member firm which offers to buy and sell the securities for which it is registered. In July 2001 there were 33 market makers active on AIM.

A nominated broker must also provide the market with information on its client company via the Stock Exchange Alternative Trading Service ("SEATS PLUS", the Exchange's trading platform for AIM securities), in accordance with the Exchange's specifications from time to time.

Any member firm of the Exchange may act as a nominated broker, subject to any requisite authorisation by any other regulator. Applicants for membership, which may be partnerships, corporations, other legal entities or sole practitioners, will need to satisfy the Exchange that they have sufficient knowledge, experience and resources to carry out their

The AIM Rules

proposed functions. A list of current member firms is available on the Exchange's website, www.londonstockexchange.com. There is also a separate list of brokers who have already been appointed by AIM Companies on the Exchange's website.

(f) *Settlement arrangements (Rule 32)*: an AIM Company must ensure that appropriate settlement arrangements for its securities are in place. This is the mechanism by which a buyer's money is exchanged for the securities and the new owner is registered. In particular, except where the Exchange otherwise agrees, AIM securities must be eligible for electronic settlement. UK registered companies may be participants in the CREST settlement system. CREST was introduced in July 1996 and is an electronic, paperless form of settlement system operated by CRESTCo Limited. A company which joins CREST enables its shareholders to hold their shares without share certificates, although shares may still be held in certificated form if preferred.

A shareholder may hold shares within CREST in one of three ways:

(i) as a "full" member of CREST, provided the shareholder has the technological capacity to be linked with CRESTCo Limited. In this case the member's name will appear on the company's register of members;

(ii) as a "sponsored" member. The member's name will appear on the register but the member is not required to be linked to CRESTCo Limited, since the sponsor, who is likely to be a broker or fund manager, will charge a fee to provide this link; or

(iii) as a client of a member or sponsored member (the "nominee"). In this case the nominee's name will appear in the company's register.

A UK company may join CREST by passing a board resolution by virtue of the enabling legislation provided by the Uncertificated Securities Regulations 1995 (SI 1995 No. 3272). The company's shareholders must be notified in accordance with its articles of association of the resolution either before or within 60 days of its being passed.

The CREST contact details are: CRESTCo Limited, 33 Cannon Street, London, EC4M 5SB, www.crestco.co.uk, (Tel: 020 7849 0000). Application is normally made by the nominated adviser, in advance of the application for Admission.

The Exchange will grant derogations from the requirement to be eligible for electronic settlement in only the most exceptional circumstances, such as where none of the current electronic systems can cope with settling the AIM Company's securities, or where the local law to which the AIM Company is subject prohibits such settlement.

(g) *Fees (Rule 33)*: an AIM Company must pay the fees as set by the Exchange from time to time. An admission fee (as at July 2001 £5,000), plus VAT, if appropriate, is payable by all applicants for admission to AIM. The fee is payable no later than three business days (any day upon which the Exchange is open for business) before admission of the Applicant Co's securities to trading on AIM. A further admission fee is payable where an enlarged entity seeks admission to AIM following a reverse takeover under Rule 13 of the AIM Rules.

As at July 2001, the annual fee for an AIM Company was £5,000, plus VAT, if appropriate. The annual fee is billed in the first week of January for the 12 months commencing 1 January and must be paid within 30 days of the invoice date. Companies joining AIM after 30 September 2001 will not be charged an annual fee for 2002. The Exchange cannot confirm whether this arrangement will apply for subsequent years.

The fee is not refundable, either in whole or in part, should the admission of AIM securities of an AIM Company to trading on AIM be cancelled before the end of the relevant year.

Information on paying fees may be obtained from the AIM team on 020 7797 4154.

3.2.2 *Suitability for Admission*

The nominated adviser must be satisfied that, in its opinion, an Applicant Co and its securities are appropriate to be admitted to AIM (Rule 34 and Schedule Six).

The nominated adviser is likely to require that:

(a) the company has reached a stage of development where a substantial market for its products is demonstrable;

(b) the core management team of the company has been with it for some time and built an infrastructure for growth; and

(c) substantial profitability is in prospect in the short term (say, within a year of joining the market).

Occasionally, new companies with exceptional prospects, often in the field of high technology, will be admitted on the basis of projected earnings and profitability.

3.2.3 Re-organisation and rationalisation of share structure

To comply with the above requirements, and to meet market expectations, a company is likely to undertake certain preparatory steps in the months prior to Admission. For instance, a review is likely to be undertaken of the company's corporate structure, including any other members of its group. A UK company which is not already a public company will have to re-register as one, which requires shareholder approval and a minimum allotted share capital of £50,000. It is also likely that, prior to Admission, there will need to be some corporate re-organisation, which may involve moving assets or businesses around within the group and/or a rationalisation of the share structure of the company whose shares are being admitted to AIM. Some companies, particularly those which have obtained venture capital finance, have different securities in issue, such as preference shares, warrants and loan stock. The different classes of shares are almost invariably re-organised into one class of ordinary shares, with the aim of ensuring that there is a single class of shares trading on AIM, that the share price on Admission is appropriate, and that there are sufficient numbers of shares in issue to allow future liquidity. A firm of registrars will be appointed to maintain the company's share register.

The re-organisation of the company's share capital will require shareholders' consent which, depending on what is being done, is likely to involve the passing of special or extraordinary resolutions at shareholders' meetings or class meetings. Lack of harmony between shareholders or different classes of shareholders may hinder the Admission process.

Where an overseas company intends to apply for Admission, local legal and regulatory issues will have to be addressed. For instance, the method of transferring shares in the overseas company may not be compatible with the AIM market and there have been instances of UK holding companies being set up and their shares admitted to trading on AIM to address this.

3.2.4 Additional pre-Admission arrangements

A company coming to AIM will often adopt one or more employee share schemes, such as share option schemes. Existing schemes should be reviewed to ensure that they comply with institutional guidelines and current law and practice. The executive directors should have service contracts, and companies often need to adopt new Articles of Association in a form appropriate for a listed company.

Particularly if a company or its group has a long history, it will be necessary to carry out a due diligence review, under which lawyers acting for the company, together with its accountants, will investigate its legal arrangements and financial information and procedures, with a view to satisfying the nominated adviser that the affairs of the company and its group are in order. The process will also elicit information to be incorporated into the Admission Document – the document which is required to be produced on Admission and which is used to market shares to investors (*see* Appendix 1 of this Guide for a model Admission Document). This work will also assist the verification exercise carried out on the information contained in the Admission Document.

3.3 Directors and employees

3.3.1 Role of directors

A director of an AIM Company has an important role in ensuring that the company operates in a proper manner and complies with its obligations under the AIM Rules. As the onus is on the company

The AIM Rules

under the AIM Rules to ensure that the directors fulfil their obligations, the board of a company coming to or on AIM should consider whether its directors' service contracts should contain provisions requiring compliance with those obligations. In particular, it would be good practice for such service contracts to be terminable and to provide for a director to leave the board, if the director materially breaches or causes the company materially to breach the AIM Rules. However, the company would need to consider carefully whether or not to exercise the right to terminate if the situation arose.

In interpreting the AIM Rules, it should be borne in mind that the Glossary defines a "director" as a person who acts as a director, whether or not officially appointed to such position.

3.3.2 *Lock-ins (Rule 7)*

An Applicant Co must, where it has as its main activity a business which has not been independent and earning revenue for at least two years, ensure that all persons who are, at the time of its Admission, its related parties and applicable employees, agree not to dispose of any interest in the Applicant Co's AIM securities for a period of one year from the date of Admission. Such agreement will be evidenced by a written undertaking by each person affected. The purpose of this restriction is to protect investors by ensuring that a company's management do not simply use Admission as a means of realising their investment in the company, and nominated advisers may seek to impose a longer lock-in period and require other significant shareholders to retain their shares. The meanings of the terms "related party" and "applicable employee" are described in the Glossary attached to the AIM Rules.

A related party is a director of any member of an AIM Company's group (defined by reference to parent/subsidiary undertakings) or a substantial shareholder (a person who holds any direct or indirect legal or beneficial interest in 10 per cent or more of any class of AIM security of the AIM Company or 10 per cent or more of the voting rights of the AIM Company) or an "associate" (as defined in the Glossary definition of "related party") of any of those. It should be noted that in the definition of "substantial shareholder" it is stated that Rule 7 does not apply to a substantial shareholder who is either an authorised person (a person who, under European Union directive or UK domestic legislation, is authorised to conduct investment business in the UK) or a company with securities quoted upon the Exchange's markets. The Exchange will also not require a substantial shareholder to be subject to the lock-in where that shareholder became a substantial shareholder at the time of the AIM Company's Admission and at a price which was more widely available.

An applicable employee means any employee of an AIM Company, or its subsidiary or parent undertaking, who together with that employee's family has any legal or beneficial interest, whether direct or indirect, in 0.5 per cent or more of a class of AIM securities. For these purposes, the following are treated as family members: the employee's spouse, any child under 18 and any trust in which the employee or such individuals are trustees or beneficiaries and any company over which they have control of more than 20 per cent of its equity or voting rights in general meeting. Any employee share or pension scheme where such employee or such individuals are beneficiaries rather than trustees is not taken into account.

The restrictions contained in Rule 7 are intended to apply to the interests of such family members as well as those of the relevant applicable employee.

Rule 7 will not apply:

(a) in the event of an intervening court order;

(b) if a party subject to the Rule dies; or

(c) in respect of an acceptance of a takeover offer for the AIM Company which is open to all shareholders.

The Guidance Notes recommend that to minimise the risk of parties to lock-in arrangements subsequently being deemed to constitute concert parties under the City Code on Takeovers and Mergers, Applicant Cos or their advisers may wish to consult the Panel on Takeovers and Mergers, London Stock Exchange Tower, London EC2P 2JX (Tel: 020 7382 9026) prior to drafting any lock-in agreement.

3.3.3 Notifying change in directors (Rule 15)

An AIM Company must notify the CAO without delay of the resignation or dismissal of any director or the appointment of any new director giving the date of such occurrence and, in the case of an appointment, the details required by paragraph (f) of Schedule Two.

3.3.4 Restrictions on dealings in AIM securities (Rule 19)

Rule 19 provides that an AIM Company must ensure that its directors and applicable employees do not deal in any of its AIM securities (i.e. securities of a class which has been admitted to dealing on AIM) during a close period. This Rule is considered in more detail in Chapter 7.

3.3.5 Directors' responsibilities (Rule 27)

An AIM Company must ensure that each of its directors accepts full responsibility, collectively and individually, for the AIM Company's compliance with the AIM Rules.

3.3.6 Directors' disclosure (Rule 27)

In addition, an AIM Company must ensure that each of its directors discloses without delay all information which the AIM Company needs in order to comply with Rule 15 (disclosure of miscellaneous information), so far as that information is known to the director or could with reasonable diligence be ascertained by the director.

3.3.7 Advice from the nominated adviser (Rule 27)

An AIM Company must ensure that each of its directors seeks advice from its nominated adviser regarding the AIM Company's compliance with the AIM Rules whenever appropriate and takes that advice into account.

As the directors are under a positive obligation to continue to seek advice and guidance from the nominated adviser, they should consider whether the company's agreement with the nominated adviser should include specific obligations on the nominated adviser to update and meet with the directors on a regular basis. The nominated adviser, in turn, is likely to want to establish in the agreement who is the appropriate recipient of information at the company and to have the right to receive management information and attend board meetings, but the nominated adviser should bear in mind that it may receive unpublished price-sensitive information and take care to ensure that neither it nor any of its representatives becomes a "shadow director". A shadow director is defined in the Companies Act 1985 ("the Act") as a person in accordance with whose directions or instructions the directors of a company are accustomed to act, although a person is not deemed to be a shadow director by reason only that the directors act on advice given by that person in a professional capacity. A shadow director incurs many of the statutory responsibilities of an appointed director.

3.4　Nominated adviser

3.4.1　Role of the nominated adviser

Each company applying to be listed, and which is listed, on AIM must have appointed a nominated adviser (Rules 1 and 30) which is responsible for ensuring that the company is suitable for AIM and for compliance with the AIM Rules.

A nominated adviser is likely to be a stockbroker, investment bank, firm of accountants or other financial professional experienced in corporate finance and must be approved by the Exchange and appear on its register.

The responsibilities of the nominated adviser (as stated in Rule 34 and described in sections 3.4.7 and 3.4.8 below) are owed solely to the Exchange. The Exchange expects a nominated adviser to have frequent contacts with its AIM Companies, to brief them on changes to the AIM Rules and market practice, and to ensure that new directors understand their duties.

An AIM Company is required to notify the CAO without delay of the resignation, dismissal or appointment of its nominated adviser or nominated broker (Rule 15). The Guidance Notes with respect to Rule 15 state that where an AIM Company needs to announce the loss of its nominated adviser it should first liaise with AIM Regulation (Tel: 020 7797 4404) so that where no replacement nominated adviser has been appointed the necessary suspension pursuant to Rule 30 may be put in place to coincide with the announcement.

The Guidance Note on Rule 34 states that on detailed regulatory matters the Exchange will only liaise with AIM Companies or their nominated advisers and on a named basis.

3.4.2 Register of nominated advisers (Rule 34)

Only an adviser whose name appears on the register of nominated advisers maintained by the Exchange may act as a nominated adviser. The list of nominated advisers as at July 2001 is provided at the back of this Guide. The current register of nominated advisers is available on the Exchange's website at www.londonstockexchange.com.

3.4.3 Eligibility criteria – obtaining approval as a nominated adviser

A firm wishing to be included on the Exchange's register of nominated advisers must comply with the eligibility criteria for nominated advisers provided by the Exchange in a document entitled "*Nominated adviser eligibility criteria*".

This document sets out the minimum criteria for approval as a nominated adviser, which are in addition to any legal or regulatory authorisation required by an applicant in any jurisdiction in which it operates. The Exchange emphasises that in assessing the suitability of an applicant to become a nominated adviser, its overriding consideration will be the preservation of the reputation and integrity of AIM. The Exchange reserves the right to decline an application notwithstanding that an applicant otherwise meets its minimum criteria.

3.4.3.1 Minimum criteria

An applicant seeking approval as a nominated adviser must:

(a) be a firm or company (individuals are not eligible);

(b) have practised corporate finance for two years;

(c) have acted as the principal corporate finance adviser in three "relevant transactions" during that two-year period; and

(d) employ at least four "qualified executives".

The Exchange states that it may at its sole discretion waive the requirement for a two year track record where the applicant has highly experienced qualified executives: it cites the example where substantially the entire team of qualified executives transfers from an existing nominated adviser.

3.4.3.2 "Qualified executives"

A qualified executive is defined as a full-time employee of an applicant who is involved in giving corporate finance advice and who has acted in a corporate finance advisory role, which includes the regulation of corporate finance, for at least three years and in at least three "relevant transactions" – *see* section 3.4.3.3 below. An employee will not be regarded as a qualified executive by the Exchange, however, where the employee has been subject to disciplinary action by a regulator or law enforcement agency in the context of financial services or corporate finance or if, as a result of any interview which it conducts, the Exchange considers that the employee has an inadequate understanding of corporate finance, market practice or the legal or regulatory framework for corporate finance.

3.4.3.3 "Relevant transactions"

Generally qualifying transactions are defined as:

(a) transactions requiring listing particulars or a prospectus (under the European directives No. 80/390/EEC and No. 89/298/EEC) in any member state of the European Union; and

(b) takeovers of public companies within the European Union.

However, at least two of these transactions must be in respect of shares quoted on a regulated market (as defined by European Directive No. 93/22/EEC).

The Exchange will consider similar initial public offerings and other major corporate transactions for publicly quoted companies including mergers and acquisitions whether within the European Union or elsewhere in the world. The Exchange reserves the right to decide whether a transaction is relevant for the purposes of the eligibility criteria, and in making its assessment it will ensure that only transactions on major stock exchanges of the world are included.

The Exchange will not allow an adviser to claim any transaction as a relevant transaction unless that applicant acted as a principal corporate financial adviser and was named prominently and unequivocally as such in the public documentation relating to that transaction. Copies of this public documentation must be included with the application to become a nominated adviser.

3.4.3.4 Preservation of the reputation and integrity of AIM

The Exchange reserves the right to reject an applicant, even though it otherwise meets the minimum criteria, if the approval of the applicant may endanger the reputation or integrity of AIM.

In considering whether an applicant might endanger the reputation and integrity of AIM, the Exchange will examine:

(a) whether the applicant is adequately regulated;

(b) the applicant's standing with its regulators;

(c) the applicant's general reputation;

(d) whether the applicant or its executives have been the subject of adverse disciplinary action by any legal, financial or regulatory authority;

(e) whether the applicant is facing such disciplinary action; and

(f) insofar as relevant, the commercial and regulatory performance of its clients to whom it has given corporate finance advice.

3.4.3.5 Application process

An applicant seeking approval as a nominated adviser must complete and submit to the Exchange an application form (Form NA1) together with an application fee which is non-refundable unless an application is withdrawn prior to "gazetting" (publicising the application – see below). As at July 2001, the application fee was £10,000 exclusive of VAT.

The Exchange will conduct interviews of some or all of the employees put forward by an applicant in its application form to ensure that they have sufficient understanding of corporate finance, market practice and the regulatory and legal framework for the applicant to be approved as a nominated adviser. Such interviews will be conducted in London and accommodation, travel and other costs will be at the applicant's own expense.

At least 14 days before the Exchange makes its decision whether to approve an applicant, it will:

(a) release publicly through the Exchange's Regulatory News Service ("RNS") the applicant's name and those of its employees cited in its application form; and

(b) where an applicant operates mainly outside the UK, the Exchange will in addition issue a newspaper advertisement in a leading domestic financial newspaper in the jurisdiction in which the applicant is registered or in which it operates stating that the applicant has made application to become a nominated adviser on AIM and inviting any objections.

This procedure is described as gazetting and the Exchange will take into account any objections which it receives as a result of the public disclosure of the applicant's name.

Prior to the public release of such information an applicant may ask the Exchange privately for an informal preliminary indication of whether, at that stage, the Exchange considers that there could be difficulties in the applicant being approved. The applicant may then withdraw its application. If the applicant withdraws in these circumstances, the Exchange will refund half of the application fee.

The AIM Rules

An applicant will be informed privately in writing of the decision of the Exchange whether or not to approve it as a nominated adviser. The notification of approval will include a list of the nominated adviser's employees which the Exchange has accepted as qualified executives.

A decision of the Exchange may be appealed publicly by an applicant (but not an individual executive) to an appeals body in accordance with the latest published version of the Exchange's "Disciplinary Procedures and Appeals Handbook".

3.4.4   *Eligibility criteria – ongoing obligations of a nominated adviser*

3.4.4.1   *Independence*

A nominated adviser must be able to demonstrate that both it and its executives are independent from the AIM Companies for which it acts such that there is no reasonable basis for impugning its independence. Where the Exchange requires a nominated adviser to demonstrate clearly that neither its independence nor that of any of its executives has been or will be compromised by any potential conflict of interest, the burden of proof will be upon the nominated adviser. In cases of doubt about its independence, a nominated adviser should consult the Exchange in advance of entering into any arrangements.

A nominated adviser may not act as both reporting accountant and nominated adviser to an AIM Company unless it has satisfied the Exchange that appropriate safeguards are in place.

3.4.4.2   *Wider conflicts of interest*

A nominated adviser must not have and must take care to avoid the semblance of a conflict between the interests of the AIM Companies for which it acts and those of any other party. In particular, a nominated adviser must not act for any other party to a transaction or takeover other than its AIM client company.

3.4.4.3 Obligations under the AIM Rules

The nominated adviser must at all times abide by its responsibilities under the latest edition of the AIM Rules.

3.4.4.4 Proper procedures

A nominated adviser must ensure that it maintains procedures which are sufficient for it to discharge its ongoing obligations under the eligibility criteria. In particular, it must ensure that any members of staff who are not approved as qualified executives are properly supervised by those who are so approved.

3.4.4.5 Adequacy of staff

A nominated adviser must ensure that it has sufficient corporate finance staff to discharge its obligations as a nominated adviser under the eligibility criteria at all times. In assessing whether it has sufficient staff a nominated adviser must have regard to the number and type of AIM Companies for which it acts. As a minimum, however, the nominated adviser must retain at least four qualified executives who would have sufficient experience for that nominated adviser to be approved were it a new applicant.

3.4.4.6 Ongoing experience of corporate finance

A nominated adviser must ensure that it continues to meet the minimum approval criteria for nominated advisers. In particular, a nominated adviser must have been involved in sufficient recent relevant transactions to allow it to qualify were it a new applicant at any time. The Exchange reserves the right to conduct further tests to ensure that qualified executives maintain an understanding of corporate finance and the responsibilities of being a nominated adviser.

3.4.4.7 Maintenance of records

A nominated adviser is required to retain sufficient records to maintain an audit trail of the advice which it has given to the AIM Companies for which it acts as nominated adviser. Such records must be retained for at least three years.

3.4.4.8 Annual Fees

A nominated adviser must pay the annual fee set by the Exchange. As at July 2001 the annual fee for a nominated adviser was £4,000 plus VAT. The fee is billed in the first week of January for the 12 months commencing 1 January and must be paid within 30 days of the invoice date. The annual fee for the first year (up to 1 January of the following year) is payable on approval of the application to become a nominated adviser. The fee is for each year or part thereof and is not refundable in the event that the nominated adviser is removed from the register.

3.4.4.9 Changes in qualified executives

Application to have further employees registered as qualified executives may be made to the Exchange at any time using Form NA2. A nominated adviser must notify the Exchange in writing without delay if any of its qualified executives leaves its full-time employment.

3.4.5 Eligibility criteria – monitoring performance

3.4.5.1 Performance review

The Exchange may subject a nominated adviser to a formal review to ensure that it has fully discharged its responsibilities under the eligibility criteria. The nominated adviser must ensure that its qualified executives co-operate fully with the Exchange and that the appropriate partner or director for a transaction is available to answer any questions by the Exchange about that transaction. The nominated adviser must allow Exchange officers access to its records and business premises when so requested by the Exchange.

3.4.5.2 Removal of qualified executives

A qualified executive leaving the full-time employment of a nominated adviser will cease to be regarded as its qualified executive. The Exchange may remove an employee as a qualified executive for a nominated adviser where that employee:

(a) is subject to bankruptcy;

(b) is subject to disciplinary action by another regulator;

(c) is mentally incapacitated; or

(d) has been shown by a formal review of the nominated adviser by the Exchange to have failed to act with due skill and care in relation to his or her employer's role as a nominated adviser.

The nominated adviser or the qualified executive may appeal against a decision to disqualify that executive in accordance with the procedures set out in the latest published version of the Exchange's "Disciplinary Procedures and Appeals Handbook".

3.4.5.3   Disciplinary action against a nominated adviser

If the Exchange considers that a nominated adviser is either in breach of its responsibilities under the eligibility criteria or under the AIM Rules, or has failed to act with due skill and care, or that the integrity and reputation of AIM has been or may be impaired as a result of its conduct or judgement, the Exchange may:

(a) censure the nominated adviser;

(b) remove it from the register of nominated advisers; and/or

(c) publish the action it has taken and the reasons for that action.

These sanctions are reiterated in Rule 38 of the AIM Rules (*see* section 3.6.4 below).

3.4.5.4   Moratorium on acting for further AIM Companies

Where, in the opinion of the Exchange a nominated adviser has insufficient staff and/or is appealing against disciplinary action taken by the Exchange, the Exchange may prevent that nominated adviser from acting as a nominated adviser for any additional AIM Companies until that situation is resolved to the Exchange's satisfaction.

The AIM Rules

3.4.5.5 Appeals by nominated advisers

Where the Exchange takes any steps against a nominated adviser pursuant to the eligibility criteria or the AIM Rules, that nominated adviser may appeal against the Exchange's decision in accordance with the procedures set out in the latest published version of the Exchange's *"Disciplinary Procedures and Appeals Handbook"*.

3.4.6 Nominated adviser's agreement

An agreement setting out the terms of engagement will be entered into between the nominated adviser and the Applicant Co or AIM Company. It will usually address *inter alia* the following provisions:

(a) *The responsibilities of the nominated adviser with respect to Admission*: the nominated adviser will usually undertake some, if not all, of the following responsibilities with respect to Admission:

   (i) assistance with the appointment and co-ordination of the company's advisers, including its solicitors, reporting accountants, brokers, public relations advisers and registrars;

   (ii) an evaluation of the company's organisational structure and strategy, and assistance with its presentations to potential investors;

   (iii) liaising with the company's legal advisers on the reorganisation of its share capital into a single class of ordinary shares;

   (iv) co-ordinating the drafting of the Admission Document;

   (v) involvement in the verification process;

   (vi) an evaluation of fund-raising options;

   (vii) valuation of the company and pricing of the issue of shares on Admission (in conjunction with the nominated broker); and

(viii) acting as the company's agent in arranging for the placing of its newly issued shares on Admission (the detailed terms of which are usually provided for in a separate Placing Agreement).

(b) *Continuing duties*: the nominated adviser will agree to act as such on a continuing basis after Admission and its responsibilities (most of which also apply to the Admission process) are likely to include the following:

(i) advising and guiding the company as to compliance with the AIM Rules;

(ii) advising the company in relation to the requirement for and timing of any circulars, announcements, accounts or other financial information required to be released or published under the AIM Rules;

(iii) liaison with the Exchange on behalf of the company;

(iv) if relevant, acting as nominated broker; and

(v) when reasonably required by the company, advising the company on investment conditions and the marketing and/or pricing of the company's securities.

(c) *Provision of information*: the company will usually undertake to provide the nominated adviser with all relevant material information and documents in a timely manner, and to keep the nominated adviser fully informed of all strategies, developments and discussions that are relevant to its engagement, and to discuss in advance all relevant initiatives. The nominated adviser should bear in mind that it may receive unpublished price-sensitive information.

(d) *Compliance with law and regulation*: the company should undertake that it and its directors will comply with all relevant legal and regulatory requirements, in particular the AIM Rules, and will do whatever else the nominated adviser reasonably requires to allow the nominated adviser to carry out properly its responsibilities.

The AIM Rules

(e) *Announcements*: the company and the nominated adviser are likely to agree that no public announcements will be made or public documents despatched by either of them with respect to the company without either consulting with, or obtaining the authorisation of, the other.

(f) *Confidentiality*: usually the nominated adviser will undertake to maintain the confidentiality of any confidential information which it receives with respect to the company; and the company will usually agree to keep confidential the information provided, advice given and views expressed by the nominated adviser in connection with its appointment, subject in each case to appropriate exceptions.

(g) *Indemnity*: the company will indemnify the nominated adviser and its associates from any liability incurred in connection with its appointment, subject to certain exceptions which will invariably include liability arising as a result of the negligence (or gross negligence), fraud or wilful default of the nominated adviser or its associates, or breach of contract or their regulatory duties by any of them.

(h) *Conflicts of interest*: the agreement usually acknowledges that the nominated adviser may find itself in situations where there is a conflict of interest between the interests of the company and the interests of the nominated adviser and its group, or those of its other clients and that the nominated adviser may retain the relevant profits and fees.

(i) *Fees*: the agreement will usually provide for the nominated adviser to be entitled to:

  (i) a fee for assisting with the preparations for Admission;

  (ii) a commission for arranging for the placing of the company's shares on Admission (if applicable); and

  (iii) reimbursement of the nominated adviser's expenses, including legal fees, and other expenses with respect to Admission.

The nominated adviser will also charge an annual fee with respect to its continuing role as nominated adviser.

A Practitioner's Guide to the Alternative Investment Market Rules

(j) *Termination*: in view of the consequences of a company ceasing to have a nominated adviser (*see* section 3.6.1 below), usually the company will want the nominated adviser to give at least one to three months' notice of termination (and the nominated adviser is likely to require the company to give similar notice), typically after an initial fixed term period of one year or more, although both parties may reserve the right to terminate immediately if the other (including any director in the case of the company) is in material breach of any legal or regulatory requirement or standard, or in the case of the nominated adviser if it is removed from the register of nominated advisers maintained by the Exchange.

(k) *Warranties*: the nominated adviser may obtain short-form warranties from the company.

The requirements of any regulatory authority or body to which the nominated adviser is subject should be borne in mind when drafting the agreement.

3.4.7 Nominated adviser's responsibilities on admission of securities (Rule 34)

The nominated adviser is required to confirm to the Exchange in writing in such form as the Exchange may from time to time prescribe (there is a form of declaration provided by the Exchange) that in relation to any application for admission of securities to AIM which requires the production of an Admission Document the following criteria set out in Schedule Six to the AIM Rules (as elaborated in the form of declaration) are satisfied:

(a) the directors of the company have received satisfactory advice and guidance (from the nominated adviser or other appropriate professional advisers) as to the nature of their responsibilities and obligations to ensure compliance by the company with the AIM Rules and the Rules of the Exchange as amended from time to time;

(b) to the best of the knowledge and belief of the nominated adviser, having made due and careful enquiry, all relevant requirements of the AIM Rules (save for the Admission Document's compliance with Regulation 9 of the POS Regulations – general duty of disclosure) have been complied with; and

The AIM Rules

(c) in the nominated adviser's opinion, it is satisfied that the company and the securities which are the subject of the application are appropriate to be admitted to AIM.

The nominated adviser must lodge its declaration at least three business days (any day on which the Exchange is open for business) before the expected date of admission of the securities to trading on AIM (Rule 5).

The Exchange has also stated that for the purpose of fulfilling the obligations owed to the Exchange, it is expected that nominated advisers will satisfy themselves that an appropriate due diligence/verification exercise has been carried out on an Applicant Co.

3.4.8 Nominated adviser's further obligations (Rule 34)

In addition, the nominated adviser is required to be available at all times to advise and guide the directors of an AIM Company for which it acts as to their obligations to ensure compliance by the AIM Company with the AIM Rules on an on-going basis. The nominated adviser must also advise the Exchange if it ceases to be the AIM Company's nominated adviser. These matters are also confirmed and elaborated on in the form of declaration by the nominated adviser referred to in section 3.4.7 above, which in addition contains a confirmation that the nominated adviser will comply with the AIM Rules applicable to it in its role as nominated adviser, as required by Rule 34. A nominated adviser must submit a declaration in respect of any AIM Company for which it takes over the role of nominated adviser (Rule 34) and in respect of an enlarged entity seeking admission to AIM following a reverse take-over (Rule 13).

Rule 34 also requires the nominated adviser to provide to the Exchange such information in such form and within such time limits as the Exchange may reasonably require and to review regularly with the AIM Company the AIM Company's actual trading performance and financial condition against any profit forecast, estimate or projection included in the AIM Company's Admission Document or otherwise made public on behalf of the AIM Company in order to assist the directors of the AIM Company in determining whether an announcement is necessary under Rule 15 (notification of any material change between the AIM Company's actual trading performance or financial condition and any profit forecast, estimate or projection included in the Admission Document, or otherwise made public on behalf of the AIM Company).

Finally, Rule 34 requires a nominated adviser to liaise with the Exchange where requested to do so by the Exchange or an AIM Company for which it acts and to abide at all times by the eligibility criteria described in sections 3.4.3 to 3.4.5 above.

A further specific responsibility in the Rules for a nominated adviser is contained in Rule 12, which requires the independent directors of an AIM Company entering into a material related party transaction to have consulted the nominated adviser in reaching an opinion as to whether the terms of the transaction are fair and reasonable so far as the holders of the AIM securities of the AIM Company are concerned.

3.5 Publication and disclosure of information

3.5.1 Wide powers to require publication (Rule 20)

The Exchange has wide powers to require an AIM Company to provide information, and may at any time:

(a) require an AIM Company to provide to the Exchange such information in such form and within such time limit as the Exchange considers appropriate; and

(b) require an AIM Company to publish such information.

3.5.2 The Exchange's power to make disclosure (Rule 21)

The Exchange may disclose any information in its possession:

(a) to co-operate with any person responsible for supervision or regulation of financial services or for law enforcement;

(b) to enable it to discharge its legal or regulatory functions, including instituting, carrying on or defending proceedings; or

The AIM Rules

(c) for any other purpose where it has the consent of the person from whom the information was obtained and, if different, the person to whom it relates.

3.6 Sanctions

The Exchange considers it important that the AIM Rules are carefully observed, not only to build investor confidence in the companies on AIM, but also for the protection of investors and the credibility of the market as a whole.

3.6.1 Failure to have a nominated adviser (Rule 30)

If an AIM Company ceases to have a nominated adviser, this must be announced (Rule 15) and the Exchange will suspend trading in its AIM securities. If within one month the AIM Company has failed to appoint a replacement nominated adviser, the admission of its securities to trading will be cancelled. Where an AIM Company needs to announce the loss of its nominated adviser, it should first liaise with AIM Regulation (Tel: 020 7797 4404) so that where no replacement has been appointed the necessary suspension may be put in place to coincide with the announcement. Where a new nominated adviser is appointed, an announcement will be required under Rule 15 and a new nominated adviser declaration (*see* sections 3.4.7 and 3.4.8 above) should be submitted to the Exchange under Rule 34.

The Rules previously provided that the same consequences (suspension and cancellation) would follow if an AIM Company ceased to have a nominated broker. The Exchange removed the reference to the nominated broker in September 1998, so that an AIM Company is not necessarily suspended immediately upon the loss of its nominated broker, in order to allow the Exchange to take account of the particular circumstances of each case in deciding appropriate action. An AIM Company's agreement with its nominated broker should still, as with a nominated adviser's agreement, have a suitable notice period.

3.6.2 Investor protection (Rules 35 and 36)

The Exchange may suspend the trading on AIM of AIM securities in the following circumstances:

(a) where trading in those securities is not being conducted in an orderly manner;

(b) where the Exchange considers that an AIM Company has failed to comply with the AIM Rules;

(c) where required for the protection of investors; or

(d) where the integrity and reputation of the market has been or may be impaired by dealings in those securities.

Suspensions are effected by a dealing notice involving an announcement being delivered to the CAO for distribution to the public through the Exchange's RNS.

The Exchange will cancel the admission of securities to trading on AIM where those securities have been suspended from trading for six months. Cancellations are also effected by a dealing notice in the same way.

3.6.3 Disciplinary action against an AIM Company (Rule 37)

If the Exchange considers that an AIM Company has contravened the AIM Rules, it may take the following measures:

(a) fine it;

(b) censure it;

(c) publish the fact that it has been fined or censured; and/or

(d) cancel the admission of its AIM securities.

3.6.4 Disciplinary action against a nominated adviser (Rule 38)

If the Exchange considers that a nominated adviser is in breach of its responsibilities under Rule 34, or has not acted with due care and skill, or that the integrity and reputation of AIM has been or may be impaired as a result of the conduct or judgement of the nominated adviser, the Exchange may:

(a) censure the nominated adviser;

(b) remove the nominated adviser from the list of approved nominated advisers maintained by the Exchange; and/or

(c) publish what action it has taken and the reasons for that action.

If action is taken against a nominated adviser by the Exchange, it may also result in disciplinary proceedings being brought by the nominated adviser's regulator.

3.6.5 *Disciplinary process (Rule 39)*

Where the Exchange proposes to take any of the steps described in Rules 37 and 38 it will follow the procedures set out in its "*Disciplinary Procedures and Appeals Handbook*".

3.6.6 *Appeals (Rule 40)*

Any decision of the Exchange in relation to the AIM Rules may be appealed to an appeals committee in accordance with the procedures set out in the Exchange's "*Disciplinary Procedures and Appeals Handbook*" which is available from the Secretary to the appeals committee.

Chapter 4
THE ADMISSION DOCUMENT AND THE APPLICATION PROCEDURE

Tom Mackay
Partner – Head of ABC Corporate
Jennifer Carter Shaw
Partner
Amhurst Brown Colombotti

4.1   Introduction

When a company applies for the admission of its securities to trade on AIM, it must:

(a) appoint a nominated adviser;

(b) appoint a nominated broker;

(c) publish an Admission Document; and

(d) comply with certain other administrative requirements set out in the AIM Rules for Companies ("the AIM Rules") published by London Stock Exchange plc ("the Exchange") including the payment of a fee and the submission of certain information and application forms.

Certain information and documents must be provided to the Exchange in advance of admission. A model timetable and list of documents are provided in Appendix 2 and 4 to this Guide.

The Admission Document must contain the same information which would be required to be included in a prospectus (whether or not the new applicant is offering securities to the public in the UK). The Public Offers of Securities Regulations 1995 ("the POS Regulations") prescribes the content of an offer of securities to the public (in a prospectus) in the UK.

4.2 The Admission Document

A model Admission Document for an offer for the subscription of ordinary shares to the public is provided in Appendix 1 to this Guide. It contains the information required by the Exchange to be published by companies seeking admission to AIM. It is important to note that this document is intended only as a starting point for the initial discussion draft and will be subject to much amending and updating; specific legal advice should be sought in the preparation of any Admission Document or prospectus.

In addition to the information required by the POS Regulations, the AIM Rules provide that the Admission Document must:

(a) contain a risk warning about AIM prominently and in bold (on the first page);

(b) contain a working capital statement;

(c) where it contains a profit forecast, estimate or projection:

   (i) contain a statement by the directors that the forecast, estimate or projection has been made after due and careful enquiry;

   (ii) contain confirmation from the nominated adviser that it has satisfied itself that the forecast, estimate or projection was made after due and careful enquiry by the directors;

   (iii) include a statement of the principal assumptions for each factor which could have a material effect on the achievement of the forecast, estimate or projection. The assumptions must be specific and clearly written to ensure investors readily understand them;

(d) in the case of a company whose main activity is a business which has not been independent and revenue earning for at least two years, contain a statement that the directors, employees, and if the company or its holding company or subsidiaries and their associates, families or trusts (except those who hold any interest of less than ½ per cent) have agreed not to dispose of any interests in their AIM shares for a period of one year from the

The Admission Document and the Application Procedure

date of admission (save in the event of an intervening court order, a takeover offer open to all shareholders becoming unconditional or death);

(e) contain information relating to each director (including shadow directors) and each proposed director including full name and age, the names of all companies and partnerships of which the director has been a director or partner at any time in the previous five years, details of any receiverships, compulsory liquidations and creditors' voluntary liquidations of any company where such director was a director at the time of, or within 12 months preceding, such events and details of certain convictions and public criticisms;

(f) contain the names of any person (excluding professional advisers disclosed in the Admission Document and trade suppliers) who either has received within 12 months before admission to AIM, or will receive after admission to AIM, fees or benefits totalling £10,000 or more, or securities in the company with a value of £10,000 or more;

(g) contain the name of any person who, in so far as is known to the issuer, is interested directly or indirectly in three per cent or more of the company's capital.

Investing companies are required to publish details of investment strategies in the Admission Document.

The Exchange may refuse admission to AIM if the applicant has not complied with any special conditions which the Exchange considers appropriate. The Exchange may also authorise the omission of information from the Admission Document.

If a company seeking admission to AIM already has a class of securities listed on AIM, then it does not need to publish an Admission Document unless it is required to do so under the POS Regulations.

The Admission Document must be published by making copies of it available, free of charge, to the public at an address in the UK or on the internet as specified in the Admission Document from the date of admission to trading on AIM for not less than one month.

The Admission Document is not vetted in advance by the Exchange.

A model Admission Document is provided in Appendix 1 to this Guide.

4.3　　Preliminary documents

4.3.1　　List of documents

At an early stage in the admission process an Index of Documents needs to be produced for the applicant. This is a crucial control tool in the application process.

A model Index of Documents is provided in Appendix 4 to this Guide.

4.3.2　　List of parties

It is important for people to be able to contact each other quickly. One of the first documents to be prepared is a list of parties including home addresses and mobile numbers of all key persons involved in the process.

4.3.3　　Timetable

At an early stage the nominated adviser will produce the proposed Timetable. In practice, in the initial stages the directors and some advisers treat the Timetable without respect but the only way to bring about an admission within budget is to stick rigidly to an agreed timeframe.

A model Timetable is provided in Appendix 2 to this Guide.

The Admission Document and the Application Procedure

4.3.4 Letters of appointment

In order to manage the process properly it is important to reach agreement as to who is doing what. In particular it is important to agree the specific work required of the reporting accountant. In addition, letters of appointment will be required for the solicitors, nominated broker, nominated adviser, PR adviser and registrar. Depending also on the transaction, letters of appointment may also be required for actuaries, surveyors and the receiving bank.

4.3.5 Legal questionnaire

As part of the preliminary documents, the solicitors for the applicant or the nominated adviser will produce a legal due diligence questionnaire. This is part of the process of drawing out company information which will be included in the Admission Document.

4.4 Minutes and internal re-organisation

4.4.1 Share for share exchange

The applicant will have to consider its structure. Does it require any form of group re-organisation? If the company is at an early stage in its development it might not have a balance sheet that is suitable for converting into a plc. A new holding company is often put in place which acquires the existing trading company under a share for share exchange agreement; this should be programmed into the Timetable.

4.4.2 Extraordinary General Meeting ("EGM")

It is almost always necessary to have an EGM (or written resolution) prior to an Admission Document being issued. Members will be asked to authorise the directors to issue shares, disapply pre-emption rights and so on; again this may impact on the Timetable.

4.4.3 Pathfinder board meeting

Depending on whether a placing proof (sometimes called a pathfinder) is being issued, a board meeting approving that proof will be required, and whether or not a placing proof is issued a board meeting is usually held to approve the near final version of the Admission Document and to appoint a committee of the directors to deal with outstanding issues.

4.4.4 AIM board meeting

The final board meeting is required to approve the issue of the Admission Document.

Model Board Minutes are provided in Appendix 3 to this Guide.

4.4.5 Issue board meeting

After applications for allotment of the shares have been received, a board meeting must be held (at the appropriate time) to issue the shares.

4.5 Public relations

A public relations ("PR") agency will produce its own list of documents and timetable dealing with matters such as questions and answers for presentations to institutions, the public and the press. The company and its advisers will need to consider the implications of the restrictions a financial promotion contained in the Financial Services and Markets Act 2000 (the "FSMA"). Broadly speaking, the Admission Document, certain limited information relating to the Admission Document, and press releases are exempt from the financial promotion restriction, but all other information which could be construed as a financial promotion must be approved by a person authorised to do so by the FSMA.

The PR agency will also advise on, draft, electronically transmit to the Exchange, and distribute to the media and appropriate analysts all announcements made by the company. In addition, the PR agency will engage in relationship building on behalf of the company with the media, analysts and the City in general.

4.6 Placing agreement

4.6.1 *Conditionality*

The placing agreement provides for matters such as conditionality of obligations of the nominated adviser. These conditions relate to matters such as the delivery of signed documents.

4.6.2 *Obligations of the broker*

The placing agreement (unless the issue is being underwritten) will not have any onerous obligations on the part of either the nominated adviser or the nominated broker. However, the nominated broker will be required to use reasonable endeavours to arrange for investors to subscribe for the shares.

4.6.3 *Warranties*

The most crucial aspect of the placing agreement to the directors will be the warranties and undertakings given to the nominated broker/nominated adviser. These warranties may guarantee that:

(a) all statements of fact contained in the Admission Document are true and accurate in all material respects and are not misleading;

(b) the Admission Document contains all information required by, and complies with, the law;

(c) the Admission Document contains all such information as investors and their professional advisers would reasonably require, and reasonably expect to find there, for the purpose of making an informed assessment of the assets and liabilities, financial position, profits and losses, and the prospects both of the company and of the rights attaching to its share capital.

4.6.4 *Limits on warranties*

The directors will seek a limitation on the warranties. It is normal for the non-executive directors to have a reasonably small cap on their liability (but it depends on their shareholding and whether they have any real commercial interest in the company). There is often considerable debate about any cap on the liability of executive directors.

4.6.5 Time limits on warranties

There will normally be an end date for liability. This is often linked to six months after delivery of the second set of audited accounts from the date of admission. In the case of any tax claim, the time limit will normally last until six months after the sixth anniversary of the current accounting period.

4.6.6 Restrictions on disposals

The placing agreement often also contain restrictions on disposals of shares by the directors. In addition, the nominated broker may also want to require certain other parties not to dispose of their shares within a particular period. He will do this through a separate agreement – sometimes called "a restricted persons agreement".

4.7 Verification

4.7.1 Verification notes

The purpose of verification notes is to assist the directors of the company and others named in, or connected with the preparation of, the Admission Document to comply with the responsibility statement in, and generally with their legal responsibilities in respect of, the Admission Document. The verification notes provide a record of the steps which have been, or are being, taken to check the accuracy of the factual information contained in the Admission Document and the basis for every forecast, estimate or expression of opinion contained in the Admission Document.

In particular, verification notes are intended to ensure that, with a view to protecting the directors and others, no incorrect statement is made (for instance, because one or more persons involved in preparing the Admission Document believes that some other person has checked that statement); the implications that the reader might reasonably draw from factual statements in the Admission Document are justifiable; and due consideration has been given to every forecast, estimate or expression of opinion.

The Admission Document and the Application Procedure

4.7.2 Directors' responsibilities

However, each director should appreciate that he takes individual responsibility (as well as collective responsibility with the other directors) for the whole Admission Document and for ensuring that all relevant facts are disclosed in the Admission Document.

In addition, a director should particularly bear in mind that Section 397 of the FSMA makes it a criminal offence (punishable by a fine or imprisonment, or both) to make a statement, promise or forecast which he knows to be (or is reckless about whether it is) misleading, false or deceptive, or dishonestly to conceal any material facts for the purpose of inducing (or being reckless as to whether it may induce) someone to acquire or dispose of investments, or to refrain from doing so. Generally "reckless" means without care or due regard to reasonably foreseeable risk.

The directors must believe, and have reasonable grounds for believing, that each material statement of fact or opinion in the Admission Document is true and not misleading, and that taken as a whole it gives a true and fair view of the history, business and prospects of the company and nothing has been omitted so as to make the Admission Document misleading in any material respect. It is important to note that it is not sufficient to claim that a particular statement taken on its own is strictly true; that statement also must not be misleading in the context in which it appears.

The verification notes do not attempt to cover every statement in the Admission Document or every implication arising from those statements. Therefore it is very important that the whole Admission Document is carefully considered and approved by, or on behalf of, each director, bearing in mind the standard of care required of them by law.

4.7.3 Documentary and third party evidence

Where possible, documentary evidence should be produced in support of the reply to each question asked or in support of the confirmation sought (even where it is not explicitly requested), and a copy of such evidence should be attached to the verification notes. Answers should be given with references to authoritative sources, either from the company's own records or, where appropriate, from outside. If evidence or confirmation of any matter has been obtained from a person other than a director this should be from a person, firm or body that is fully qualified or experienced in the relevant field; such evidence or confirmation should be on the basis of an original opinion or original research, and not reported confirmation or hearsay.

When it is stated that the directors rely on another person, this is understood to mean that each director agrees that it is reasonable to rely on that other person. Although there are some verification matters which could reasonably be delegated by the directors to third parties, the directors should appreciate that such delegation will not relieve the directors of their personal responsibility to ensure that each matter is correctly stated in the Admission Document.

4.7.4 *Confidentiality and scope of verification notes*

The verification notes are treated as confidential and are not made public or put on display.

The verification notes do not purport to verify, other than minimally, the accountants' report or other reports and reviews, each of which is the primary (though not exclusive) responsibility of the firm which signs it.

4.8 Financial due diligence

4.8.1 *Long-form report*

The nominated adviser has to give instructions to the reporting accountants as to what is required. He should detail what form of report is required; in particular he should specify any areas of concern.

4.8.2 *Board memorandum on financial reporting procedures*

The nominated adviser will normally require a letter from the directors stating that the company has adequate financial reporting procedures to permit an accurate assessment of the financial position; a board memorandum will set out the basis on which the statement is made.

The Admission Document and the Application Procedure

4.8.3   Working capital memorandum

The Admission Document must contain a statement by the directors that in their opinion, "having made due and careful enquiry", the working capital available to the company and its group is sufficient for its present requirements. This is not a requirement of the POS Regulations but only of the AIM Rules. This working capital statement has material cost implications as the directors will probably need to obtain an accountants' report on the company's working capital.

4.8.4   Report on any profit forecast, estimate or projection

Most professional advisers would prefer not to include illustrative projections in any document with which they are associated on the basis that the history of prospectuses shows how wrong such projections can be. When dealing with professional investors it is often sufficient to set out the opportunity and leave it to the professional investor to analyse what the opportunity might be worth. However, when dealing with private investors it is often thought necessary to give more information. Additional information is required in the Admission Document wherever it expressly, or by implication, states a minimum or maximum for the likely level of profits or losses for a period subsequent to that for which audited accounts have been published, or if it contains data from which a calculation of an approximate figure for future profits or losses may be made, even if no particular figure is mentioned and the words "profit" or "loss" are not used. Further details of the requirements are set out in the model Admission Document (*see* Appendix 1 to this Guide).

4.8.5   Indebtedness statement

While not a specific Admission Rule, the Admission Document commonly contains an indebtedness statement. This shows loan capital, term loans, all other borrowing (including acceptance credits, hire purchase commitments and obligations under finance leases), and the total amount of any contingent liabilities or guarantees of the group. Normally the Rules of the Official List are followed and the indebtedness statement date is not more than 42 days prior to the date of publication of the Admission Document.

4.8.6 Estimate of expenses of issue

The nominated adviser will keep a running total of estimated expenses which should, prior to the issue of the Admission Document, be approved by the board. This will include the fees for the nominated adviser, the nominated broker, the company's solicitors, the nominated adviser's solicitors, PR agents, printers and the Exchange.

4.9 Directors

4.9.1 Directors' questionnaires

Many directors of AIM companies have been entrepreneurs for a number of years and inevitably some of their business ventures have been failures. It is vitally important that appropriate disclosure of the directors' histories is made in the Admission Document. While the AIM Rules focus on disclosure and there is no requirement to submit directors' questionnaires, in practice the nominated adviser will require the directors to complete a questionnaire about themselves. The professional advisers will carry out searches on the directors with the Registrar of Companies who has been working with the Insolvency Service of the Department of Trade and Industry to improve the availability of information about directors.

4.9.2 Memorandum on the responsibilities and liabilities of directors

This sets out the background law, the persons responsible for the Admission Document, the contents of the Admission Document (including the overriding duty of disclosure under Regulation 9 of the POS Regulations), and other areas of civil and criminal liability. There will also be a memorandum on the duties and responsibilities of the directors. As part of the application procedure to the Exchange, the nominated adviser has to confirm that the directors have received guidance as to the nature of their responsibilities and obligations, and this memorandum is part of that process.

4.9.3 Responsibility letter signed by directors

While the directors will sign off the verification notes (and also normally a final copy of the Admission Document), it is common to ask the directors to sign off a detailed letter acknowledging their responsibility for various items appearing in the Admission Document.

4.9.4 Powers of attorney signed by each director

Once the process is nearing completion, the costs and the urgency involved mean that there can be no delay caused by the absence of a director. It is therefore common for each director to execute a power of attorney authorising any co-director to sign on his behalf any document required for the Admission Document or to complete the application procedure.

4.9.5 Directors' service agreements

It is normal for directors' service contracts to be negotiated when preparing the Admission Document. While the director may seek increased remuneration, the company and its advisers will want to ensure the tightest possible contract in terms of intellectual property rights and restrictive covenants.

4.9.6 Share option schemes

It is common for share option schemes to be set up when preparing the Admission Document. A decision needs to be taken as soon as possible as to the appropriate type of scheme to be adopted. Schemes range from Enterprise Management Incentives ("EMI") schemes, Inland Revenue approved schemes and unapproved schemes. EMI schemes are the easiest to implement and offer significant tax advantages although there are certain formal requirements such as the requirement for the company to have gross assets of less than £15 million. Only employees may join EMI or approved schemes whereas non-executives and consultants may join unapproved schemes. Specialist advice should be sought to enable the right schemes to be set up as quickly as possible.

4.9.7 Dealing code

Before being admitted to AIM, a company must ensure that all directors and any employees holding (together with their associates) ½ per cent or more of the company's shares do not deal in those shares during a close period. The adoption of a suitable dealing code to regulate dealings must be documented appropriately. *See* Chapter 6 of this Guide for further information on close periods and dealing requirements.

4.10 Tax

The Admission Document will contain one or two paragraphs on taxation; these sections will need to be cleared by a tax lawyer or tax accountant.

Internal re-organisations are common immediately prior to the publication of the Admission Document. These re-organisations are normally arranged so as to have a neutral tax effect. There is an advance clearance mechanism, but it is important to note that the Revenue takes up to 30 days to respond to an application for advance clearance; this should be built into the Timetable.

4.11 Insurance

As part of the due diligence process, a nominated adviser may well request a letter from the insurance brokers confirming that the company is appropriately insured.

4.12 Application to the Exchange

4.12.1 Ten-day information

An issuer seeking admission to AIM for any class of securities for the first time must notify the Exchange of the following matters at least ten business days prior to the expected date of admission to AIM:

(a) the name, registered office and country of incorporation of the issuer;

(b) a brief description of the issuer's business;

The Admission Document and the Application Procedure

(c) the number and nature of the securities and whether capital will be raised on admission;

(d) the full names and functions of the directors (including any shadow directors) and the proposed directors of the issuer;

(e) insofar as it is known to the issuer, the name of any person who is interested in three per cent or more of the issuer's capital together with the amount of the issued share capital, expressed as a percentage, of each person's interest;

(f) the names and addresses of any persons who will be disclosed in the Admission Document as receiving fees, benefits or securities of more than £10,000 (excluding professional advisers named in the Admission Document);

(g) the anticipated accounting reference date;

(h) the name and address of the nominated adviser and, if different, of the nominated broker; and

(i) that the Admission Document will be available from the issuer at the time of admission and will contain full details of the company and its securities.

4.12.2   Three-day information

Not less than three business days prior to the expected date of admission to AIM, the issuer must submit an application for admission to AIM to the Exchange with six copies of the Admission Document. The application form, which has to be signed by a duly authorised officer of the company, contains a declaration relating to such matters as the working capital, any profit forecast, estimate or projection, and the company's financial procedures.

4.12.3   Charges

The issuer must pay charges for admission to AIM and on-going charges, as published by the Exchange from time to time.

4.12.4 Additional documentation

In addition to the Admission Documents and the application form, the Exchange requires a declaration signed by the nominated adviser and a letter from the nominated broker confirming his appointment. The nominated adviser has to confirm, *inter alia*, that:

(a) the directors have received guidance as to the nature of their responsibilities and obligations;

(b) to the best of his knowledge and belief, all relevant requirements of the AIM Admission Rules (save for compliance with Regulation 9 of the POS Regulations) have been complied with; and

(c) he is satisfied that, in his opinion, the Company and its securities are "appropriate" to be admitted to AIM. This latter requirement is a 1997 rule change by the Exchange and, although in itself a defensible requirement, is part of the "regulatory creep" which is pushing up the costs of joining AIM.

4.12.5 Admission

The admission of securities to trade on AIM becomes effective when the Exchange issues a dealing notice.

Chapter 5
CONTINUING OBLIGATIONS AND TRANSACTIONS

Ann Kennedy
Partner
Deloitte & Touche

5.1   Introduction

Once the applicant's shares have been admitted to AIM, there are numerous continuing obligations with which the issuer must comply. These include disclosure of financial and price-sensitive information, rules governing transactions undertaken and further share issues.

This Chapter sets out the continuing obligations of an AIM Company with regard to transactions and on a day-to-day basis.

5.2   Company Announcements Office

Information that is required to be disclosed by the AIM Rules must be disclosed to the Company Announcement Office ("CAO") of the London Stock Exchange plc ("the Exchange") without delay and no later than it is published elsewhere.

An AIM Company ("AIM Co") must take reasonable care to ensure that any information it notifies to the CAO is not misleading, false or deceptive and does not omit anything likely to affect the import of such information.

It is presumed that information notified to the CAO is required by the AIM Rules or other legal or regulatory requirements. Any information that is notified to the CAO may be deemed to be price-sensitive; "drip-feeding" of non price-sensitive information into the marketplace via CAO announcements is not allowed.

Information, which is notified to the CAO, must be in English and in writing. Methods, which may be used to transmit the information to the CAO, include fax and electronic link. Advice on formatting HTML regulatory announcements can be obtained from the Exchange website.

When notifying information to CAO, companies should follow the Regulatory News Service Guidelines published by the Exchange.

Any document provided by AIM Co to the holders of its AIM securities, must be made available to the public at the same time for at least one month, free of charge, at an address notified to the CAO. Three copies of the document must be sent to the Exchange.

5.3 General disclosure obligations

5.3.1 *Price-sensitive information*

AIM Co must notify the CAO without delay of any new developments, concerning a change in its financial condition, sphere of activity, business performance or expectation of performance, which are not public knowledge and, if made public, would be likely to lead to a substantial movement in the price of its AIM securities.

AIM Co need not notify the CAO about impending developments or matters in the course of negotiation. It may give this information in confidence prior to any announcement to certain parties including its advisers, representatives of its employees or trades unions acting on their behalf and statutory or regulatory bodies or authorities.

However, in all cases AIM Co must be satisfied that such confidants are aware that they must not trade in its AIM securities before the relevant information is announced.

If AIM Co has reason to believe that a breach of confidence has occurred, or is likely to occur, it must notify the CAO with at least a warning announcement to the effect that it expects shortly to release information which may lead to a substantial movement in the price of the AIM securities.

Continuing Obligations and Transactions

Where such information has been made public, AIM Co must notify that information to the CAO without delay, notwithstanding the fact that the CAO should be provided with all announcements before they are published elsewhere.

Information that is required to be notified to the CAO must not be given to anyone else (except as set out above) before it has been so notified. Where potentially price-sensitive information is to be announced at a meeting of holders of AIM Co's AIM securities, arrangements must be made for that information to be notified to the CAO no later than the announcement is made to the meeting.

The Exchange monitors the share prices of all fully listed and AIM Companies. It is common for the monitoring team to contact the nominated adviser if AIM Co's share price moves by more than about 10 per cent over a short period. In such cases, the Exchange will ask the company and its advisers to consider whether any announcement is necessary under the AIM Rules.

5.3.2   *Material change*

A material change between AIM Co's actual trading performance (or financial condition) and any profit forecast, estimate or projection which has been included in an admission document or otherwise made public on AIM Co's behalf should be notified to the CAO. One of the nominated adviser's responsibilities is to review regularly with AIM Co its actual trading performance and financial condition against any such profit forecast, estimate or projection in order to help AIM Co to determine whether such an announcement is necessary.

In practice, it can be difficult to assess the likelihood of a material change since shortfalls in the short term may be rectified in the medium term, so the directors' assessment of future results may be as important as historical management information. As a general rule, a deviation of more than 10 per cent from previously published indications could be regarded as a material change for these purposes.

Furthermore, a deviation of more than 10 per cent from market expectations of results could be regarded as a material change which should be disclosed as price-sensitive information. For AIM Companies which have no broking research, market expectations can be difficult to determine. Factors to consider in these cases include general press comment, as well as interim and annual reports and trading statements by the company.

5.3.3 Substantial share interests

AIM Co must notify the CAO without delay of any relevant changes to any significant shareholders, disclosing the information specified in Schedule 5 of the AIM Rules.

Sections 198 to 208 of the Companies Act 1985 ("the Act") provides the mechanism to assist in complying with the changes to significant shareholders. This requires that where a person knows that he has acquired or ceased to have a material interest of three per cent of the issued share capital of AIM Co, or already has three per cent or more of AIM Co's share capital and he increases or reduces his interest across one full percentage point, then he must notify AIM Co within two business days.

If AIM Co becomes aware of a change in a substantial interest, which should have been disclosed under Sections 198 to 208 of the Act, details must be notified to the CAO by the end of the business day following the day of receipt of the information by AIM Co. Such information might for example come to AIM Co's attention as a result of a request pursuant to Section 212 of the Act.

Section 212 of the Act allows AIM Co to send a notice to a person to confirm whether or not they have had an interest in AIM Co's share capital at any time within the past three years and to disclose details of their holding, whether they are part of a concert party or to whom their interest was sold.

In addition, AIM Co and transactions in AIM Co's securities will be subject to the Rules Governing Substantial Acquisitions of Shares and the City Code on Takeovers and Mergers, which may accelerate the speed with which AIM Co is notified of any change in its shareholders.

Continuing Obligations and Transactions

5.3.4 Director's deals

Details of any changes in the interests of the directors of AIM Co and their families in the AIM securities must be notified to the CAO without delay, disclosing the information specified in Schedule 5 of the AIM Rules. Where such a change occurs during a close period (*see* section 5.8.4), further details are required and these are also set out in Schedule 5 of the AIM Rules. In practice this must be made by the end of the business day following notification of the change.

The duty of disclosure extends to any dealing (including the grant, acceptance, acquisition, disposal, exercise of discharge) by a director, and his family, in any option relating to AIM Co's securities, or any interest in such option.

Sections 324 to 328 of the Act provides a mechanism to assist in complying with the requirement to notify the CAO of changes to director's holdings. These Sections relate to a director's duty to disclose to AIM Co his shareholdings and those of his spouse and children under 18, in AIM Co, together with the grant or exercise of options in AIM Co.

An AIM Company which is not subject to the Act is nevertheless subject to the same disclosure requirements as referred to above.

5.3.5 Board changes

AIM Co must notify the CAO of the resignation or removal of any director, or the appointment of any new director. In the case of an appointment, AIM Co is required to disclose the information on the new director set out in Schedule 2(f) of the AIM Rules. This information includes current and past (within five years) directorships and partnerships held, details of any receiverships/compulsory liquidations etc. of any company or partnership where the director was a director or partner at the time or in the 12 months preceding such events and details of any public criticisms, censures, unspent convictions and disqualifications from being a director.

5.3.6 Change of nominated adviser or broker

AIM Co must notify the CAO of the resignation, dismissal or appointment of its nominated adviser or broker. If an issuer ceases to have a nominated adviser the Exchange will suspend trading in its securities. It is advisable therefore, to establish a period of notice of at least one month on the engagement of a nominated adviser in order to avoid the potential suspension of shares.

5.3.7 Change in the number of securities in issue

AIM Co must notify the CAO of the reason for the issue or cancellation of any AIM securities. Any changes in the number of shares in issue requires liaison with AIM Regulation, so that they can arrange the appropriate dealing notice to be released.

5.3.8 Decision on dividend payment

AIM Co must notify the CAO of any decision to make any payment in respect of its AIM securities, specifying the net amount payable per security, the payment date and the record date. This information may be given in the preliminary statement of annual results or the half-yearly report if appropriate.

5.3.9 Other general disclosure obligations

The Exchange may require AIM Co to provide it with such information in such form and within such time limit as it considers appropriate and to publish such information.

The Exchange may disclose any information in its possession:

(a) to co-operate with any person responsible for supervision or regulation of financial services or for law enforcement;

(b) to enable it to discharge its legal or reulatory functions, including instituting, carrying on or defending proceedings; and

(c) for any other purpose where it has the consent of the person from whom the information was obtained and, if different, the person to whom it relates.

5.4 Financial reporting

5.4.1 Publication of annual accounts

AIM Co must publish annual audited accounts prepared in accordance with UK or US Generally Accepted Accounting Practice or International Accounting Standards. These accounts must be sent to the holders of the AIM securities without delay (i.e. once they are finalised and reported on) and in any event no later than six months after the end of the financial period to which they relate.

The Exchange will suspend AIM Companies that are late in publishing their half-yearly statement or their annual accounts. The CAO must be notified of the publication of annual audited accounts and as with any document sent to shareholders, the annual accounts must be available to the public at the same time for at least one month free of charge at an address notified to the CAO. Three copies of the annual accounts must be sent to the Exchange.

Although it is common practice for AIM Companies to publish a preliminary statement of annual results, there is no requirement to do so.

5.4.2 Publication of half-yearly report

AIM Co must prepare a half-yearly report within three months of the end of the relevant period and all reports must be notified to the CAO.

Although there is no specific requirements for the contents or layout of the half-yearly report, best practice is to follow the standards set for fully listed companies. *The Accounting Standards Board's Statement on Interim Reports* published in September 1997 recommends principles for interim financial reporting. The figures need not be audited but best practice is to follow Cadbury Code guidance: the interim report should be reviewed by the auditors, who should discuss their findings with the audit committee.

In addition to the figures (which normally comprise the profit and loss account, balance sheet, and cash flow statement, together with comparative figures for the corresponding period in the preceding financial year), the half-yearly report would be expected to contain an explanatory statement covering the figures and an indication of the group's prospects for the current financial year. It is advisable to ensure that the indication of the group's prospects cannot be construed as a profit forecast because that might give rise to an obligation to make further disclosure at a later date.

A profit forecast would include any form of words which expressly or by implication give a floor or ceiling for the likely level of profits or losses for the current financial year, or which contain data from which a calculation of an approximate figure for future profits or losses may be made, even if no particular figure is mentioned and the word profit is not used.

When making profit forecasts consideration should also be given to the requirements of Section 47 of the Financial Services Act 1986. Under that Section any person who: (a) makes a statement, promise or forecast which he knows to be misleading, false or deceptive, or dishonestly conceals any material facts; or (b) recklessly makes (dishonest or otherwise) a statement, promise or forecast which is misleading, false or deceptive; is guilty of an offence if he makes the statement, promise or forecast, or conceals the facts for the purpose of inducing, or is reckless as to whether it may induce, another person to enter or offer to enter into, or refrain from entering, or offering to enter into, an investment agreement, or to exercise, or refrain from exercising, any rights conferred by an investment.

If AIM Co changes its accounting reference date such that the accounting period is extended AIM Co must prepare further reports for each subsequent six-month period expiring prior to the new accounting reference date.

For example, if the year-end is changed from 31 December to 31 March such that there is a 15-month accounting period, AIM Co must prepare audited accounts for the year ended 31 December X1, then interim reports for the six-month periods ended 30 June 19X2 and 31 December 19X2, followed by audited accounts for the 15 months ended 31 March 19X3.

Continuing Obligations and Transactions

5.5 Transactions

Certain transactions carried out by AIM Co are "classifiable" and may require disclosure and in some cases shareholder approval. A classifiable transaction is any transaction that is **not** either:

(a) of a revenue nature and in the ordinary course of business; or

(b) an issue of securities, or a transaction to raise finance, which does not involve the acquisition or disposal of any fixed asset of AIM Co or its subsidiary undertakings.

Examples of classifiable transactions might include acquisitions and disposals of shares, businesses and assets, including agreed private deals and public takeovers.

If a transaction is classifiable, certain "class tests" must be applied to determine whether or not disclosure and/or shareholder approval is required. The implications for a substantial transaction, a related party transaction and a reverse takeover are set out in sections 5.5.2, 5.5.3 and 5.5.4 respectively. The varying requirements for these types of transaction mean that AIM Co and its advisers are well-advised to consider the class tests at an early stage in the planning of a proposed transaction.

5.5.1 Class tests

The class tests comprise the following percentage ratios, as set out in Schedule 3 of the AIM Rules (where detailed explanations of the calculations can be found):

(a) *gross assets*: gross assets the subject of the transaction – divided by the Gross assets of AIM Co;

(b) *profits*: profits attributable to the assets subject to the transaction – divided by profits of AIM Co;

(c) *turnover*: turnover attributable to the assets the subject of the transaction – divided by turnover of AIM Co;

(d) *consideration*: consideration – divided by aggregate market value of all the ordinary shares of AIM Co;

(e) *gross capital:* gross capital of the company or business being acquired – divided by the gross capital of AIM Co.

In circumstances where the above tests produce anomalous results or where the tests are inappropriate to the sphere of activity of AIM Co, the Exchange may (except in the case of a transaction with a related party) disregard the calculation and substitute other relevant indicators of size, including industry specific tests. Only the Exchange can decide to disregard one or more of the class tests, or substitute another test, and AIM Co or its nominated adviser should contact the Exchange at the earliest opportunity if such a dispensation is to be sought.

5.5.2 Substantial transaction

If any of the class tests is 10 per cent or more, the transaction is a "substantial transaction" and AIM Co must notify the CAO without delay as soon as the terms of the transaction are agreed. The information to be disclosed is set out in Schedule 4 of the AIM Rules which provides for detailed particulars on the transaction. The requirements are similar to those under the Listing Rules for a transaction where any of the class tests are five per cent or more but less than 25 per cent. Shareholder approval is required for listed companies wishing to perform a transaction where any of the class tests exceed 25 per cent. AIM Companies need only obtain shareholder approval at 100 per cent, which can be a factor in deciding whether AIM or a full listing is appropriate.

There is no general obligation for AIM Co to inform its shareholders directly of a substantial transaction. It may however, need to do so if shareholders are asked to vote on a related matter, for example the issue of further shares by AIM Co. It may also wish to do so for investor and public relations purposes.

5.5.3 Related party transaction

Where any transaction whatsoever with a related party exceeds five per cent in any of the class tests, AIM Co must notify the CAO without delay disclosing the information set out in Schedule 4 of the AIM Rules, the name of the related party concerned and the extent of their interest in the transaction and a statement that its

Continuing Obligations and Transactions

independent directors consider, having consulted with its nominated adviser, that the terms of the transaction are fair and reasonable insofar as the holders of its AIM securities are concerned.

This contrasts with a fully listed company which would require a circular to shareholders and shareholder approval for a related party transaction.

Details of any transaction with a related party (including the identity of the related party, the consideration and all other relevant circumstances) where any class test exceeds 0.25 per cent must be included in AIM Co's next published accounts, whether or not notified to the CAO as described above. Thus if all tests are less than five per cent but at least one is greater than 0.25 per cent, this is the only disclosure which needs to be made.

5.5.4 Reverse takeovers

A reverse takeover is an acquisition or acquisitions in a 12-month period which for AIM Co would:

(a) exceed 100 per cent in any of the class tests;

(b) result in a fundamental change in its business, board or voting control; or

(c) in the case of an investing company, depart substantially from the investment strategy stated in its admission document.

A reverse takeover will require shareholder consent and disclosure to the CAO without delay of the information set out in Schedule 4 of the AIM Rules and insofar as it is with a related party, the additional information required for related party transactions.

Unless the subject of the transaction is fully listed or on AIM, upon receiving shareholder approval trading in the AIM securities of AIM Co will be suspended. If the enlarged entity seeks admission, it must make an application in the same manner as any other applicant applying for admission of its securities for the first time. It will need to submit a further fee, admission document, nominated adviser declarations and a company application form at least three days prior to admission. However, the new entity may make an application in advance of the general meeting to approve the reverse takeover such that the securities are admitted on agreement of the acquisition.

Where AIM Co is unable to publish its admission document at the same time as it agrees the terms of a reverse takeover, it will be suspended by the Exchange until it has published such a document (unless the target is a listed company or another AIM Company). If the enlarged group does not seek a new admission, trading in the AIM securities of AIM Co will be cancelled.

5.5.5 Aggregation of transactions

Transactions completed during the 12 months prior to the date of the latest transaction must be aggregated with the latest transaction for the purpose of classifying that transaction, where:

(a) they are entered into by AIM Co with the same person or persons or their families;

(b) they involve the acquisition or disposal of securities or an interest in one particular business; or

(c) together they lead to the principal involvement in any business activity or activities which did not previously form a part of AIM Co's principal activities.

5.6 Further share issues

A further admission document will be required for AIM Co only when it is:

(a) required to issues a prospectus under the Public Offers of Securities Regulations 1995 ("the POS Regulations") for a further issue of AIM securities;

(b) seeking admission for a new class of securities; or

(c) treated as an applicant following a reverse takeover.

The Exchange may authorise the omission of information from a further admission document in the same circumstances as apply for first time applicants under Rule 4. In addition, AIM Co may omit

Continuing Obligations and Transactions

specified information (paragraphs 41 to 47 of the POS Regulations) from any further admission document where further AIM securities are offered on a pre-emptive basis to some or all of the existing holders of such securities provided that AIM Co has been complying with the AIM Rules. In such circumstances the nominated adviser to AIM Co must confirm to the Exchange in writing that equivalent information is available publicly by reason of AIM Co's compliance with the AIM Rules.

AIM Co is exempted from preparing a further admission document which would be required by the above where less than 10 per cent of a class of AIM securities are being offered and AIM Co has been complying with the AIM Rules. In such circumstances, the nominated adviser to AIM Co must confirm to the Exchange in writing that equivalent information is available publicly by reason of AIM Co's compliance with the AIM Rules.

At least three business days before the expected date of admission of further AIM securities, AIM Co must submit an application form and where required, any further admission document.

5.7 The City Code on Takeovers and Mergers

If AIM Co is itself the subject of a takeover approach (or the directors are considering seeking a buyer for the company) it should be noted that the City Code on Takeovers and Mergers is likely to apply to the transaction. This, in particular, will be the case for companies which are considered to be resident in the UK, the Channel Islands or the Isle of Man.

5.8 Other eligibility requirements and restrictions

5.8.1 *Continuing eligibility*

Once admitted to AIM, AIM Co must continue to satisfy the initial eligibility criteria. In particular, it must at all times retain a nominated adviser and a broker.

5.8.2 Nominated adviser

If AIM Co ceases to have a nominated adviser the Exchange will suspend trading in its securities. It is advisable therefore, to establish a period of notice of at least one month on the engagement of a nominated adviser in order to avoid the potential suspension of shares.

5.8.3 Broker

AIM Co must retain a broker at all times and must ensure that appropriate settlement arrangements are in place, in particular (unless otherwise agreed with the Exchange), AIM securities must be eligible for electronic settlement.

5.8.4 Director's share dealing

In addition to the restrictions of the Criminal Justice Act 1993 to prevent insider dealing when in possession of unpublished price-sensitive information, an AIM Co must ensure that its directors and applicable employees (those employees with 0.5 per cent or more of a class of AIM Co's AIM securities) do not deal in any of its AIM securities during a close period (the period of two months immediately preceding the preliminary announcement of the company's annual results or half-yearly report, or when the company is in possession of unpublished price-sensitive information).

This rule will not apply, however, where such individuals have entered into a binding contract prior to the close period where it was not reasonably foreseeable at the time when such commitment was made that a close period was likely and provided that the commitment was notified to the CAO at the time it was made.

The Exchange may permit a director or applicable employee to sell his AIM securities during a close period to alleviate severe personal hardship such as the need for a medical operation or to satisfy a court order where no other funds are readily available.

5.8.5 Transferability of shares

AIM Co must ensure that its AIM securities are freely transferable except where any jurisdiction, statute or regulation places restriction on transferability or AIM Co is seeking to ensure that it does not become subject to a statute or regulation if it has a particular number of shareholders domiciled in a particular country.

5.8.6 Securities to be admitted

Only securities which have been unconditionally allotted can be admitted as AIM securities. AIM Co must ensure that application is made to admit all securities within a class of AIM securities.

5.8.7 Fees

AIM Co must pay the fees as set by AIM at the rates published by the Exchange. The current rates (excluding VAT) are £5,000 admission fee and £5,000 annual fee for issuers, and £10,000 admission fee and £4,000 annual fee for nominated advisers.

5.8.8 Directors responsibility for compliance

AIM Co must ensure that each of its directors: (a) accepts full responsibility, collectively and individually, for its compliance with the AIM Rules; (b) discloses without delay all information which it needs in order to comply with Rule 15 of the AIM Rules (insofar as that information is known to the director or could with reasonable diligence ascertained by the director); and (c) seeks advice from its nominated adviser regarding its compliance with these rules whenever appropriate and takes that advice into account.

Chapter 6
THE TRADING RULES

John Wakefield
Director and Head of Corporate Finance
Rowan Dartington & Co Limited

6.1 Introduction

The AIM Company ("AIM Co") has been successfully admitted to trading on AIM. An investor – whether a private individual or institutional fund manager – intending to buy or sell shares in AIM Co is likely to be concerned with three main issues: price, payment and delivery. How do investors find out about AIM Co, in particular how shares are bought and sold, and the practicalities of dealing on AIM?

This Chapter examines the trading and regulatory environment in which shares in AIM Co are traded and which regulate the trading activities of the market practitioners – the nominated adviser, the nominated broker and the market maker.

6.2 The SEAT PLUS system

Information on AIM quoted shares is disseminated by the SEATS PLUS trading system ("Stock Exchange Alternative Trading System") which is operated by the London Stock Exchange plc ("the Exchange") in conjunction with third party service providers, such as Reuters and Datastream / ICV. SEATS PLUS is an extension of the SEAQ system. SEAQ stands for Stock Exchange Automated Quotations and is used by Exchange member firms for publishing the prices of listed securities. A SEAQ security is a domestic equity market security for which a minimum of two market makers displays two-way prices and for which there is a "normal market size" (i.e. the minimum quantity of securities in which the market makers are obliged to quote a firm two-way price).

SEATS PLUS is used to provide similar information on SEATS securities, defined by the Exchange Rules as "non SEAQ" securities, including all AIM quoted securities. SEATS PLUS is used for publishing prices and information on securities in which there is only one or no market maker prepared to quote two-way prices. In practice this means thinly traded, fully listed securities as well as all AIM securities irrespective of their size or liquidity.

The principal difference between SEAQ and SEATS PLUS is that the member firm making a market in SEAQ securities must make a firm two-way price in a minimum quote size during the mandatory quote period (08.00 – 16.00 during days on which the Exchange is open for business). With the SEATS PLUS system, the market maker is not obliged to make firm prices and may choose to show indicative prices only at a level at which it may be prepared to deal. In practice, as Winterflood Securities has undertaken to make a market in all AIM stocks, there is always a firm price quoted for AIM companies, although this is not always the case for the small number of fully listed companies which are traded on SEATS PLUS.

In addition, there is a "hit order" mechanism on SEATS PLUS enabling Exchange member firms to execute deals electronically, simply by accepting the published bid or offer price. The "hit order" facility is only available where prices are quoted firm – that is, by reference to a limit in terms of a specified size and price (a "limit order"). This should not be confused with the "order book" trading facility, SETS ("Stock Exchange Electronic Trading in Securities"), which was introduced in October 1997, initially for trading in those SEAQ securities which are included in the FTSE 100 and which is being gradually extended to highly liquid SEAQ securities, such as those comprised in the FTSE 250, which tend to attract four or more market makers.

6.3 Information requirements

The Exchange requires the following information to be provided for AIM Co securities via SEATS PLUS:

(a) the date the information was last updated;

The Trading Rules

(b) the SEDOL ("Stock Exchange Daily Official List") or ISIN ("International Securities Identification Number") code;

(c) the industry sector;

(d) the number of shares in issue;

(e) the approximate free market capital ("FMC") as a percentage of shares in issue; FMC excludes shares owned by directors, connected persons (*see* Section 326, Companies Act 1985 ("the Act")), and shareholders owning five per cent or more;

(f) the expected dates of announcement of preliminary and interim results;

(g) the company's final or interim turnover, whichever is later;

(h) the net interim and (if available) final net dividend figure;

(i) the volume of shares traded in the last 12 months; and

(j) the volume of shares traded to date during the current month.

This information is usually input by the nominated broker.

A typical page on an AIM traded security, as published by Reuters, is as follows:

```
Printed by Reuters: John Wakefield                            Friday 22 June 2001 16:14:00
SSY.L           SCIENCE SYSTEMS        XD   Cls    540-580
SEAQ  GBp
NMS   1         PL  6                                         GMT  15:11
                                   Net  0     H 550          L 545
Vol   48.1                                                   News
Last         ↑550        D550        D545
Order Book                                                   0/0
    Price  Agg  Size  Bid Code       Price Agg Size Offer Code

                                                             3/3
          NITE  PEEL  WINS       540-580     WINS PEEL NITE
NITE      540-580         1x1    07:57  WINS  540-580  1x1    07:44
PEEL      540-580         1x1    07:46
```

The example shows that Science Systems has three market makers – Knight Securities ("NITE"), Peel Hunt ("PEEL") and Winterflood Securities ("WINS"). All are making a market in 1,000 shares (the normal market size) at 540–580. The "bid" price is therefore 540p and

A Practitioner's Guide to the Alternative Investment Market Rules

the "offer" price is 580p, giving a spread of 40p, which is equivalent to seven per cent of the mid-market price of 560p and from which the market makers will derive their "turn".

Any buy or sell orders – whether firm, indicative or via the "hit order" mechanism – may be shown in the spaces indicated. The example does not indicate any persons currently offering to buy or sell against firm "hit" orders.

As mentioned, Winterflood Securities has given an assurance that it will make markets in all AIM stocks. Most of the trading transacted in AIM securities is therefore undertaken in conjunction with market makers and there are relatively few orders posted under the "hit order" or bulletin board facility.

The following example is of information published by Reuters on Dinkie Heel which shows a member firm, Capel Cure Sharp, prepared to sell 100 shares at 9p per share through the hit order mechanism.

```
Printed by Reuters: John Wakefield                          Friday 22 June 2001  16:14:00
DINK.L        DINKIE HEEL PLC           Cls           8-9
SEAQ  GBp
NMS  0.5      PL 3                                                      GMT  15:11
                                        Net  0        H                        L
Vol                                                                     News
Last
Order Book                                                                   0/1
         Price  Agg Size  Bid Code            Price    Agg Size  Offer Code
                          CCMR   F            9.00     100.000   FO192HWM01

                                                                             2/1
             NITE  MLSB                       8-9      WINS
MLSB         8-9 ½           5x5   07:37      WINS     7 ½ - 9      5x5     07:36
NITE         8-9 ½           5x5   07:56
```

The bulletin board is also used in connection with Officially Listed stocks which have no market maker. The Reuters page for Chepstow Race Course gives details of the last 10 trades and shows five member firms prepared to buy at various prices and one member firm, Brewin Dolphin, prepared to sell 200 shares at £27 per share.

86

The Trading Rules

```
Printed By Reuters: Unknown                          Monday 11 June 2001  16:04:12
INDEX <SEATS01>        MAIN INDEX <UKEQ> LSE  SETN    ORDER INFORMATION         CRC/L
                                                     CORP BKR BREWIN DOLPHIN BELL LAWRIE
                                       CLOSE        PHONE STX 72393
                                                    BUYS                         TOTAL 5
LAST TRADES                                         GERDa    F   2600.00  0.025  901BJ7WP01
27NOV00   2100.00   0.066  BREW   GMID              BREW     F   2300.00  0.200  501LH83001
15DEC00   2525.00   0.059  HSDL   TETH              NEML     F   2250.00  0.100  6019RRQ101
19DEC00   2525.00   0.041  BREW   TETH              PSSL     F   2050.00  0.250  101IMD6R01
23JAN01   2550.00   0.100  GERD   TETH              LASLa    F   2025.00  0.100  AOOUZWFXOO
26JAN01   2500.00   0.400  INTR   TETH
06FEB01   2500.00   0.050  BREW   PSSL
27FEB01   2200.00   0.500  BREW   PSSL
19APR01   2400.00   0.431  BREW   NONM
24APR01   2550.00   0.150  BREW   NONM              SELLS                        TOTAL 1
21MAY01   2300.00   0.200  BREW   NONM              BREWa    F   2700.00  0.200  FO192XE901

COMPANY INFORMATION 16APR97
ISIN      GB0001907749   CCY            GBp
SECT                     PAT       114.054K
SHRS         495.513K    TVR       909.571K
FMC            34.80%    DIV        NIL/6.00
RLTS         16APR98     YVOL         4.884t
INT          16OCT98     MVOL         0.00
```

6.4 The market practitioners

One of the main benefits of AIM is the relative simplicity of the procedures governing eligibility and admission to the market ("Admission"), in contrast to the requirements of the Official List. This is also generally true of the environment in which AIM quoted securities are traded following Admission. By and large, it is up to the market practitioners to ensure a satisfactory trading environment in which the securities can be freely traded within the regulatory framework established by the Exchange.

Although the nominated adviser is responsible to the Exchange for confirming that AIM Co is "appropriate" to be admitted to AIM and ensuring compliance by AIM Co and its directors with Chapter 17 of the AIM Rules of the Exchange ("the AIM Rules"), the nominated adviser is not required to be a member firm of the Exchange. The Trading Rules are contained in Chapter 17 of the Rules of the Exchange, (not the AIM Rules) and compliance with them is the principal responsibility of the nominated broker who is such a member firm. In addition, the (buying or selling) broker (who need not be the nominated broker) is responsible for trade reporting and settlement, generally within the CREST system (*see* section 6.8).

A Practitioner's Guide to the Alternative Investment Market Rules

6.4.1 The role of the nominated broker

By agreeing to act as nominated broker to AIM Co, the firm (an Exchange member firm) undertakes that, during the mandatory quote period, it shall upon request use its best endeavours to match bargains in AIM securities in which there is no registered market maker (Rule 17.4(b)). This means finding a willing buyer to "match" a willing seller (or vice versa), which is an order driven process rather than responding to opportunities generated by the competing quotes published by market makers.

It should be noted that, where AIM securities are traded on such a matched bargain basis, the price may not be a true reflection of market value in the absence of firm (or indicative) continuous two-way prices.

In practical terms, the nominated broker supplies liquidity by identifying and matching buyers and sellers without taking a principal position, unlike the market maker.

Three types of order for AIM securities can be input by member firms on SEATS PLUS:

(a) "firm exposure order" – where the member firm is prepared to deal at firm bid / offer prices;

(b) "indicative exposure order" – where the member firm is indicating a price and level at which it may be prepared to deal; and

(c) "hit order price" – which may be accessed automatically by member firms.

The Exchange may declare prices to be "indicative only" in certain specified circumstances and to maintain an orderly market. In addition, a firm order will be treated as indicative for a limited period of 30 minutes following an announcement by the company on the Regulatory News Service ("RNS") operated by the Exchange.

6.4.2 The role of the market maker

The defining characteristic of a security that is publicly quoted and traded on the Exchange is the presence of a market maker (previously called a "jobber" before Big Bang in 1986). A market maker is a member firm of the Exchange which wholesales lines of stock and takes a principal position by owning securities for re-sale. This enables shares to be freely traded and, as a result, the price fluctuates or "floats" according to the market makers' perception of supply and demand.

Unlike the nominated broker, who is remunerated by charging clients (buying or selling) a commission based on the value of the transaction, the market maker earns its revenue by exploiting the difference between the price at which it is prepared to buy (the "bid" price) and the price at which it is prepared to sell (the "offer" price) the shares (the "market maker's turn").

It should be noted that only a member firm that is registered as a market maker in a security can quote prices on SEATS PLUS.

Under Rule 17.11, a registered market maker in an AIM security is required to display:

(a) "firm continuous two-way prices";

(b) "indicative continuous two-way prices"; or

(c) "indicative continuous mid-prices";

in not less than the minimum quote size of 500 shares. If at least one market maker is displaying firm continuous two-way prices in a security, all market makers' prices in that security must also be "firm continuous two-way prices".

A change in the status of a price from indicative to firm requires three days' notice to the Exchange; the Exchange must be notified of a change from firm to indicative by 13.00 on the previous business day.

A market maker who changes its bid price to, or through, the limit price for which it has a sell order with a specified price and size (or changes its offer price to, or through, the limit price for which it has a buy order) is required to execute the order immediately following the change of price (Rule 17.26(d)).

Where a market maker quotes a price on the telephone that is higher than the one on display, it is obliged to deal at that price and size (Rule 17.22); where a market maker quotes a price over the telephone to another market maker in a security for which it is registered but is displaying an indicative price, that quote will be treated as firm and the market maker is obliged to deal at the quoted price (Rule 17.10(b)(ii)).

There are three control mechanisms which the market maker can use to regulate its risk in holding AIM Co securities and to encourage trading:

(a) to mark the price up and down in response to demand;

(b) to widen the bid / offer spread; and

(c) to increase or reduce the size at which it is prepared to buy or sell (but not below the minimum quote size of 500 shares).

As the market maker's income derives from its level of trading activity, its role in correctly judging market demand, relative to the number of shares on its books, is crucial both as regards its own profitability and generally in providing liquidity, thereby determining the current market value of AIM Co.

The choice and selection of a market maker is generally dealt with by the nominated broker. The nominated broker will take care to ensure that the market maker is kept informed of developments in AIM Co's trading activities and also that the market maker has an opportunity to participate in issues of new shares and significant transactions in existing shares conducted "on exchange". There are currently 24 member firms registered as market makers in AIM securities. According to Exchange statistics, 83 per cent of AIM companies have at lest two market makers (*see* London Stock Exchange Fact File 1999). At present just under 600 companies are quoted on AIM with market capitalisations ranging from under £1 million to over £800 million with the majority of companies falling within the £5 – £20 million bands. It might reasonably be concluded that there is a correlation between the size of the company and the number of market makers.

Detailed rules govern how firm and indicative orders may be executed in a particular security, depending on whether the order is "all or nothing" or a "limit order", and when the order was first given in relation to competing orders in the same security. For example, before completing a transaction, a market maker must check to see whether there are any firm exposure orders at the same price or at a more competitive price. If there are, it must satisfy the displayed order unless it is an "all or nothing" order and the proposed transaction is for a lesser number of shares with the result that the price available for completing the balance of the order would be prejudiced.

6.5 Liquidity

The price of quoted securities is driven by supply and demand which, actual or perceived, is influenced by many factors but possibly none more so than the trading performance of the company in accordance (or otherwise) with market expectations.

A great deal has been written about liquidity, or the lack of it, in AIM securities; the implication generally being that an AIM company is *per se* less liquid than a SEAQ security.

A great many influences affect liquidity, ranging from macro economic factors such as interest and exchange rates (which are outside the company's control) to sector and stock specific factors. Certainly the size of company is an important factor, if only for the reason that the largest companies tend to be more dependent on outside capital and therefore have a wider "free market capital" ("FMC") – the level of shares in the marketplace which may be considered as generally being available for trading in response to market demand – so increasing the number of shareholders and opportunities for active trading to take place.

Liquidity – the ease with which AIM shares can be freely bought and sold – is determined by the availability of shares at prices and in sizes which will attract investors wishing to deal. In practice, liquidity is supplied by the market makers' preparedness to quote continuous bid/offer prices and their willingness to do so will reflect their perception of demand for a share relative to supply in the marketplace. While investors usually want to trade shares in order to earn an investment return, the availability of shares is a function of FMC. Great care must be taken (usually the job of the nominated broker) to ensure that the supply of, and demand for, a share does not become out of kilter so that prices get distorted in relation to the underlying financial characteristics, such as price/earnings and dividend yield, by which a share is ultimately valued.

The ideal scenario is a trading environment where company performance is in accordance with, or better than, market expectations, and the FMC is such that shares are readily available for trading in response to judicious pricing by the market makers.

This creates a virtuous cycle in which there is sufficient trading activity for several market makers to provide competing quotes at the keenest prices; it is generally the environment in which FTSE 100 companies trade.

Generally speaking, it is usually the case that the smaller the company, the lower the FMC and the greater the reluctance of the market makers to make "keen" prices (which is reflected in a wide bid/offer spread) or any price at all. However, this is not seen as a function of AIM but of the size of the company in terms of market capitalisation. As a company expands, so generally does its need to access outside capital, which in turn results in the issue of further shares, so increasing the FMC.

6.6 The after-market

Liquidity is, of course, also influenced by the activity and effectiveness of the nominated broker in publicising information amongst its client-base.

The Trading Rules

Brokers take on companies where they are convinced of the prospects for above-average growth either because of the quality of the management or the products/services on offer, or market sentiment towards the sector. If brokers are unable to assess such factors, it is unlikely that they will wish to be associated with the stock and actively encourage their clients to make an investment.

So far as new issues are concerned, brokers look to price companies at a level which is designed to give investors a modest premium of around 10 per cent in initial dealings as an inducement for the risk of holding a "new" share. Ideally, the opening price should go to and remain at this level until there is an announcement justifying a price adjustment, usually the first set of figures after flotation. To maintain an active and orderly after-market, brokers will be in frequent contact with companies; estimates for the current year and future performance are updated in the light of trading conditions. Certainly, brokers would look to publish research notes following the interim or preliminary announcement of full year results as well as general and more comprehensive updates on companies following, for example, significant transactions or further capital-raising exercises.

6.7 Relations with investors

The nominated broker is responsible for maintaining an active dialogue between AIM Co and its investors who might otherwise only hear from the company on a twice-yearly basis (on publication of its interim results and preliminary announcement). The broker will also arrange institutional presentations at which the executive directors, usually the chief executive/managing director and finance director would have one-to-one meetings with the institutional shareholders.

This process is crucial if Aim Co has ambitions to raise further equity capital, such as an acquisition to be financed by an entitlement issue (rights issue or open offer) or a vendor consideration placing. In such circumstances, the broker will normally seek the agreement of the institutional shareholder that it should be made an insider prior to the commencement of such discussions which will generally be of a price-sensitive nature. In addition, the broker will seek to involve the market maker in "agency crosses" (riskless transactions in the existing shares between member firms) to allow the market maker to fulfil any limit order or to level a long or short position.

6.8 Reporting and settlement

Most transactions conducted on the Exchange are settled on CREST. CREST is the system used for settling stock exchange bargains in uncertificated (or dematerialised) form; it is operated by CRESTCo Limited (under the authority and supervision of the Bank of England) and has been operational since 15 July 1996.

CREST effectively matches all buying and selling transactions (by crediting and debiting stock and consideration electronically) to or from the buyer's or seller's account, which is operated by the 20 CREST member accounts.

The Exchange Rules require CREST trades to be reported by 21.00 on the day of the trade if the transaction was carried out during the trade reporting period (07.15 to 17.15 on days when the Exchange is open for business) or by 20.00 on the following day if it was conducted outside the trade reporting period.

Where a trade report is required, the trade must be submitted to the Exchange within three minutes of the execution of the transaction, except where it is effected outside the trade reporting period, in which case it must be reported to the Exchange between 07.15 and 08.00 during the next trade reporting period. Rule 8.19 prescribes the detailed information to be included in a trade report. All AIM transactions must be trade reported except "riskless principal transactions" (matched bargains, sometimes referred to as "agency crosses") or where the transaction is "put through" the Exchange, at the same price and size.

All risk trades are published three business days after the day of trading; riskless transactions are published as soon as the Exchange receives details.

The Trading Rules

Settlement, unless otherwise agreed, is three days after the transaction date (the date on which the transaction is effected). The minimum period for settlement on CREST is delivery on the same day, the maximum period is delivery within one year.

An alternative method of settlement is "residual settlement" (for very illiquid stocks). This involves the physical delivery of stock to the marketplace generally within three days of the transaction.

6.9   Market regulation

6.9.1   Insider dealing

6.9.1.1   Criminal liability

An individual must ensure that he does not deal in an AIM (or any publicly quoted) security on the basis of "inside information". This prohibition is, therefore, not confined to AIM and is part of the general criminal law contained in Part V of the Criminal Justice Act 1993 ("CJA").

A detailed analysis of the nature and extent of the prohibition is outside the scope of this Guide. In summary, the legislation creates an offence of "insider dealing" and prohibits the use of inside information, which may be defined generally as confidential price-sensitive information for the purposes of dealing in the securities of a quoted company and thereby deriving an advantage. The legislation, which only applies to individuals, extends beyond individuals in possession of inside information who themselves deal in the securities in question; it also applies to encouraging or procuring another person to deal, whether or not that person knows he is dealing on the basis of inside information.

The difficulty is to identify confidential price-sensitive information because much depends on the particular circumstances of each case.

Section 56 of the CJA defines "inside information" as information which:

(a) relates to a particular security or issuer, and not to securities or issuers generally;

(b) is specific or precise;

(c) has not been made public; and

(d) if it were made public would be likely to have a significant effect on the price.

According to Section 57 of the CJA, a person has information as an insider if and only if:

(a) it is, and he knows it is, inside information; and

(b) he has the information and knows that he has it from an inside source, that is from:

   (i) a director, employee or shareholder; or

   (ii) a person who has access to such information by virtue of his employment, office or profession; or

   (iii) directly or indirectly from any such person referred to in (i) and (ii).

The general principle is that any information which is not already in the public domain and can reasonably be construed as having a bearing on the value of quoted securities, and thereby requiring an announcement to be made, constitutes confidential price-sensitive information. In borderline cases, caution must be exercised and an announcement must be made before dealings take place.

Under Section 53 of the CJA, it is a defence if the individual:

(a) does not expect the dealing to result in a profit because the information is price sensitive; or

(b) believes on reasonable grounds that the information has been disclosed sufficiently widely so that no-one taking part in the transaction could be prejudiced by not having the information; or

(c) still would have dealt even if he did not have the information.

The Trading Rules

6.9.1.2 *Special defences*

Paragraph 1 to Schedule 1 of the CJA provides a defence if an individual acted in good faith in the course of his business as, or his employment in the business of, a market maker.

For these purposes, a market maker is defined as a person who "holds himself out at all normal times in compliance with the rules of a regulated market or an approved organisation as willing to acquire or dispose of securities". An "approved organisation" is defined as "an international securities self regulating organisation approved under Paragraph 25B of Schedule 1 to the Financial Services Act 1986". It therefore appears that a market maker registered as such under the Rules of the Exchange is clearly covered by this definition and so is within the scope of the defence.

6.9.1.3 *Civil liability*

In addition, it is possible to institute civil proceedings for insider trading (effectively for breach of statutory duty) with a view to obtaining restitution or compensation, as appropriate, from the defendant.

There have been remarkably few successful prosecutions and even fewer successful civil actions. Successful action under either criminal or civil law would not necessarily render the offending transaction void, voidable or otherwise unenforceable.

6.9.1.4 *Further developments*

The Financial Services and Markets Act 2000 requires the Financial Services Authority to issue a Code supplementing the statutory offences. A draft Code has been published which proposes the creation of a new offence of "market abuse". The intention appears to be to catch behaviour which is damaging to markets but which does not constitute any of the existing offences. This is in part in response to technological developments such as the wider use of the internet and increased levels of execution only trading by relatively unsophisticated individuals, which have seen instances of unscrupulous behaviour by some stock tipsters buying securities for their own account shortly before publishing "buy" recommendations.

A Practitioner's Guide to the Alternative Investment Market Rules

The provisions of the draft Code apply to all persons (individuals and corporations) and have an extra-territorial dimension in that they apply to prevent market abuse on a "prescribed market" (including the Exchange), regardless of where the abuse takes place.

6.9.1.5   Exchange requirements

For directors and relevant employees, additional constraints on dealing apply. Directors and relevant employees are considered to be particularly close to, and could therefore influence, a company's affairs as generally they are in possession of more information than is publicly available. Such individuals may, therefore, only deal with the permission of their Chairman and, in any event, are prohibited from dealing within two months prior to the publication of interim results or the preliminary announcement for the full year (or after the relevant period end has elapsed, for the period until publication of the results, if earlier).

A company joining AIM must ensure that its directors and applicable employees do not deal in its securities during a close period. A close period is any one of the following:

(a) the two month period preceding the publication of the Company's annual results (or, if shorter, the period from its financial year end to the time of publication);

(b) the two month period immediately preceding the notification of the Company's half year results (or, if shorter, the period from the relevant financial period end up to and including the time of notification);

(c) any other period when the Company is in possession of unpublished price sensitive information; and

(d) at any time when it has become reasonably probable that such unpublished price sensitive information will be required by the AIM Rules to be notified to the Company Announcements Office.

These obligations mirror those contained in the Model Code of Directors' dealings in the Listing Rules of UKLA.

The Trading Rules

It is important to emphasise that these restrictions are in addition to the criminal law which applies in all cases.

The Exchange recognises that, in certain instances, discussions will need to take place between a company looking to raise further capital (e.g. to finance an acquisition or improve its balance sheet) and its major shareholders. In these circumstances, the position is regulated by general company law and guidance can be obtained from the Listing Rules of the UK Listing Authority ("the Purple Book"). Paragraphs 9.4 and 9.5 of the Purple Book provide that, where an underwriting or capital raising by way, for example, of a selective marketing or placing is in prospect, discussions are permitted for the purposes of determining the level of support as part of the pricing mechanism between a company and its key shareholders. In practice, most firms of brokers seek to make their major institutional clients insiders, thereby depriving those shareholders of the opportunity of dealing until a full public announcement is made.

6.9.2   *Dealing announcements*

Announcement of certain transactions are required in accordance with general company law, as supplemented by the AIM Rules and the Substantial Acquisition of Shares Rules ("SARs") operated by the City Code on Takeovers and Mergers.

6.9.2.1   *Dealings by directors*

Any dealing by a director or person in whose shares the director is deemed to be interested (typically a spouse or minor children) in any "interest in shares" must be disclosed to the company within five business days and then by the company to the Company Announcement Office of the Exchange usually through the RNS operated by the Exchange no later than the next business day. The requirements of the Act are deemed not to be satisfied if certain information is excluded from the announcement, including the price and date of dealing.

6.9.2.2 Substantial interests

A person (or persons acting in concert) who acquires an interest in shares amounting to three per cent or more in a company is required under the Act to inform the company within two business days of the transaction. Thereafter, any subsequent dealing which takes the shareholder(s) through one whole percentage point, upwards or downwards, or as a result of which the shareholder(s) ceases to have a substantial interest (i.e. less than three per cent), must be reported to the company, which must then make an appropriate announcement through the RNS by the next business day.

Under Section 209(8) of the Act an interest in shares held by a market maker for the purposes of his business (only in so far as it is not used for the purpose of intervening in the management of the company) is disregarded. For these purposes a market maker is "a person authorised under the law of a member state to deal in securities and to deal on a relevant stock exchange; and [who] holds himself out at all normal times as willing to acquire and dispose of securities at prices specified by him and in so doing is subject to the rules of that exchange".

Market makers are therefore exempt from the requirement to notify companies of their substantial interests but they must nevertheless inform the Exchange; the Exchange publishes announcements via the RNS at its discretion.

6.9.2.3 Substantial Acquisition Rules

Where a person (or persons acting in concert) has acquired 15 per cent or more of the voting shares in a public company, he (they) must disclose to the Exchange any subsequent transaction which causes the shareholding to rise or fall by one whole percentage point by 12 noon on the next business day following the transaction; the Exchange then notifies the Takeover Panel which monitors compliance with the SARs.

Market makers are subject to the requirements of the SARs.

6.9.3 Integrated Monitoring and Surveillance System ("IMAS")

The Exchange operates an integrated surveillance system to monitor the London markets. IMAS is a sophisticated computer system which highlights irregularities such as large fluctuations in share prices or volumes of trades.

The system works in real-time during market hours. It monitors trades and quotes continuously and pinpoints deviations from the norm. According to Exchange statistics, IMAS identified 11,161 significant price movements in 1996, of which 1,039 merited further investigation. This should be compared with an average of over 52,000 bargains per day in UK equity securities during 1997 with more than 6.4 billion shares traded on AIM from 217,426 transactions. Liquidity on AIM has increased further, with shares to a value of over £414 million traded in 73,144 transactions in March 2001.

Generally speaking, an unexplained price movement of 10 per cent or more on one day will lead to an informal enquiry of the particular company's nominated broker by the Exchange surveillance team.

6.10 Information about AIM companies

Where does an actual or prospective investor in AIM Co look for information about the company?

There are four main sources of information:

(a) SEATS PLUS, which can be accessed by a member firm, usually a broker acting on behalf of the investor.

(b) Brokers' research notes – information prepared by corporate brokers for their private and institutional clients, include a résumé of the company and the nature of its business, an estimate of projected trading performance for the next two to three years, and a commentary on the latest published figures.

(c) Financial press – the FT publishes the latest share prices of AIM quoted companies on a daily basis. It should be noted that the price/earnings ratios ("PERs") quoted by the FT are historic as opposed to the PERs in brokers' notes. Other publications, such as *Investors Chronicle* and *AIM and Ofex News*, follow the more actively traded and fashionable AIM stocks.

(d) Published annual and interim report and accounts; the FT provides a free distribution service for many AIM companies.

As information becomes more freely available, reflecting the latest advances in technology, it is expected that the volume and scope of coverage of AIM quoted companies will increase, much of it being distributed via the Internet.

Chapter 7
DIRECTORS' DEALINGS

John Jackson
Partner
DLA

7.1 Introduction

Rule 19 of the AIM rules for companies ("AIM Rules") introduced by the London Stock Exchange plc ("the Exchange") regulates dealings in AIM securities by directors and "applicable employees" of AIM companies during a close period. The purpose of the Rule is to ensure that those bound by it (including their family) do not abuse price-sensitive information, in particular during periods leading up to the announcement of a company's results.

7.2 Directors and applicable employees

A director includes any person who acts as a director whether or not officially appointed to such position.

An "applicable employee" is an employee of the AIM Company ("AIM Co") or employee of a subsidiary or parent company of AIM Co who, together with that employees family has a holding or interest, directly or indirectly in 0.5 per cent or more of a class of securities of an AIM Company which have been admitted.

"Holding" is defined as where a person has a legal or beneficial interest (whether direct or indirect) in the AIM securities and that person is a director, an applicable employee or a significant shareholder (a holder of any legal or beneficial interest directly or indirectly in three per cent or more of any class of AIM Security).

Throughout this Chapter, references to a director should be read to include an applicable employee, as such a person must comply with Rule 19.

7.3 Dealings

The definition of "deal" includes any change whatsoever in the holding of any securities of AIM Co where the holder is a director or part of a director's family or an applicable employee. The definition also extends to:

(a) any sale or purchase or any agreement for the sale or purchase of such securities;

(b) the grant to or acceptance by such a person of an option or any other right or obligation whether present or future and whether conditional or unconditional to acquire or dispose of any such securities, the sale or purchase, exercise or discharge or any dealing with any such option;

(c) right or obligation in respect of such securities;

(d) any deals between directors and/or applicable employees;

(e) any off market deals; and

(f) any transfers for no consideration.

In the definition of deal there is specifically excluded securities where the relevant person bound undertakes or elects to take up an entitlement or actually takes up an entitlement or allows an entitlement to lapse under a rights issue or other offer (including an offer of shares in lieu of a cash dividend); or where there is a sale of sufficient entitlements nil paid to allow a take up of the balance of the entitlements under a rights issue or lastly where an undertaking to accept or accepting take-over offer is accepted.

7.4 Close period

The AIM Rules define a close period as:

(a) the period of two months preceding the publication of AIM Co's annual results or, if shorter, the period from its financial year end to the time of publication; and

(b) if it reports only half yearly, the period of two months immediately preceding the notification of its half yearly report or, if shorter, the period from the relevant financial period end up to and including the time of the notification; or

Directors' Dealings

(c) if it reports on a quarterly basis, the period of one month immediately preceding the notification of its quarterly results or, if shorter, the period from the relevant financial end up to and including the time of the notification.

Notification is defined as the delivery of an announcement to the Company Announcements Office ("CAO") for distribution to the public through the Exchange's Regulatory News Service.

(d) any other period where the AIM Co is in possession of unpublished price-sensitive information; or

(e) any time it has become reasonably probable that such information will be required by the AIM Rules to be notified to the CAO.

7.5 Unpublished price-sensitive information

The definition within the AIM Rules states that it is information which relates to a particular security or particular AIM Co rather than securities or issues in general, is specific or precise, has not been made public and if it were made public would be likely to have a significant effect on the price or value of the security of an AIM Co.

7.6 Exemptions from Rule 19

Rule 19 does not apply, however, where the director or applicable employee has entered into a binding commitment prior to the AIM Co being in a close period where it was not reasonably foreseeable at the time the commitment was made that a close period was likely, provided that the commitment was notified to the CAO at the time it was made.

The Exchange also reserves the right to permit a director or applicable employee of an AIM Co to sell its securities during a close period where it is to alleviate severe personal hardship (an example of where this might apply is where there is an urgent need for a medical operation or to satisfy a court order where no other funds are reasonably available).

7.7 Notification to the Company Announcements Office

AIM Co is required without delay to notify the CAO of any deals by directors specifying in particular:

(a) the identity of the director concerned;

(b) the date on which the disclosure was made to the CAO;

(c) the date on which the deal was effected;

(d) the price, amount and class of the security concerning;

   (i) the nature of the transaction;

   (ii) the nature and extent of the director's interest in the transaction; and

(e) where a deal takes place when it is in any close period, the date upon which any previous binding commitment was notified to the CAO or the date upon which the Exchange granted permission to deal in order to mitigate severe personal hardships.

7.8 Dealings by a director's or employees family

Under the AIM Rules the definition of family means any directors or employees spouse or child where the child is under the age of 18 years. It also includes any trust in which the director or employee is a trustee or beneficiary or any company over which they have control or more than 20 per cent of its equity or voting rights in a general meeting. However, the definition excludes any employees share or pension scheme where the individual is a beneficiary rather than a trustee.

7.9 Breach of Rule 19

If the Exchange considers that the Rule has been contravened it can:

(a) fine it;

(b) censor it;

(c) publish the fact that it has been fined or censored; and

(d) cancel the admission of AIM Co's securities.

Directors' Dealings

The Exchange also has the power to suspend the trading of AIM Co securities if it considers that the AIM Co has failed to comply with the AIM Rules such as Rule 19. However, it is more likely to want to take the measures set out above than to suspend trading.

In extreme cases the Exchange may also take action against the nominated adviser, if it believes that the breach of the Rules has come about by reason of the adviser's failure to act with due care and skill.

It will therefore be seen that a breach of the Rules by a director or applicable employee can have serious repercussions, for the company and in extreme cases its nominated adviser. A director or applicable employee who violates the Rules by disposing of shares whilst in possession of unpublished price-sensitive information may also be in breach of the insider dealing legislation which is currently set out in Part V of the Criminal Justice Act 1993.

Chapter 8
CORPORATE GOVERNANCE

John Jackson
Partner
DLA

8.1 Introduction

In 1991, as a result of a number of well-publicised cases of "Directors Behaving Badly", the then government established a committee to report on the financial aspects of corporate governance. The report, together with a code of best practice, was issued in December 1992 and became known as the Cadbury Report and the Cadbury Code respectively (taking their names from its chairman Adrian Cadbury).

In June 1993 the London Stock Exchange plc ("the Exchange") required quoted companies to include a statement in their annual report and accounts as to whether or not they were complying with the Cadbury Code.

Under the Cadbury Code, directors are required to review the effectiveness of their company's internal financial controls. Directors are required to identify the major risks facing their business and to ensure that minimum control standards are in place to identify them at the earliest possible opportunity. The Code emphasises the need for an audit committee consisting of non-executive directors.

The Cadbury Code also requires directors to report publicly that their business is a going concern – namely, that it would continue in operational existence for the foreseeable future. Whilst in itself the statement may seem innocuous, it requires the directors to consider the issue and form a view. Key to this process is the preparation and review of budgets and forecasts.

The Cadbury Code introduced other requirements:

(a) non-executive directors should bring an independent judgement to bear on issues of strategy, performance, resources (including key appointments) and standards of conduct;

(b) the majority of non-executive directors should be independent of management and free from any business or other relationship which could materially interfere with the exercise of their independent judgement (apart from their right to receive fees and to hold shares);

(c) the fees payable to non-executive directors should reflect the time which they commit to the company;

(d) non-executive directors should be appointed for specific terms, with no automatic re-appointment and executive directors' service contracts should not exceed three years without shareholder approval; as to the latter point things have moved on since the Code was first published and the current feeling of the "city" is that a period of two years and ideally one year, is now appropriate.

Since the publication of the Cadbury Code there have been two further detailed reviews into corporate governance undertaken by the Greenbury Committee and Hampel Committee.

The Hampel Committee (which was set up to review the recommendations of the Cadbury and Greenbury Committees) issued its final report in January 1998. It highlighted a need for broad principles in good corporate governance which should be applied flexibly and with common sense to the varied circumstances of individual companies. Whilst this was originally how the Cadbury and Greenbury Committees had intended their recommendations be implemented, it was felt too often that the Codes had been treated as a set of rules to which a "box ticking" approach had been taken with no regard to the different circumstances and experiences of the individual companies. The Hampel Committee felt that companies should be prepared to review and explain their corporate governance policies, including any special circumstances which in

Corporate Governance

their view justified departure from generally accepted best practice and that shareholders should be flexible in their interpretation of the Codes and should listen to the directors' explanations and judge them on their merits.

The Hampel Committee recommended that companies should include in their annual report and accounts a statement of how they have applied the relevant principles to their particular circumstances.

Interestingly, certainly as far as small companies are concerned, the Hampel Committee concluded there should be no difference between the corporate governance standards expected of larger and smaller public companies, but that the governance arrangements of smaller listed companies should be considered with flexibility and with proper regard given to individual circumstances.

8.2   What is it and why is it an issue?

How accountable is a PLC's board of directors to its shareholders? Whilst directors have a common law duty to their company to exercise reasonable care and skill, over recent years the Exchange has sought to impose further obligations. These obligations control such issues as insider dealing and disclosure of interests, and have come to be known as "corporate governance".

Whilst much of the requirements of corporate governance are entirely reasonable and require behaviour which one would expect of a Board of Directors of a public company, there is concern, certainly amongst smaller PLCs, that the labyrinth of rules and regulations calls into question their ability to do the job without having the corporate veil, as between shareholders and themselves, pierced. Recent press comment has suggested that directors should be held directly responsible for their actions, either collectively as the "board" or individually. Shareholders would have the right to sue a director for any act that could be argued to have caused a loss to the company.

From this, a growing market in directors' liability insurance will surely follow.

8.3 How does it affect AIM companies?

It does not at present but the Department of Trade and Industry ("the DTI") has indicated that it may do so before long. Moreover, if an AIM company seeks a full listing its directors need to know which corporate governance requirements apply.

8.4 What are the key issues for public limited company directors?

The Exchange has published an amendment to its Listing Particulars – the "Combined Code" of best practice on corporate governance – embracing many of the recommendations of all three Committees.

Directors will have to:

(a) state in their annual report and accounts:

  (i) the principles of the Combined Code, giving sufficient explanation to enable its shareholders to evaluate properly how the principles have been applied; and

  (ii) whether or not it has complied with the Combined Code's detailed provisions during the relevant accounting period and, if not, why not;

(b) identify which non-executive directors are independent (*see* Listing Rules 12.43(1));

(c) report on directors' remuneration (*see* section 8.5);

(d) confirm that the company is a going concern;

(e) confirm that the company has the necessary internal controls that is, financial, operational and compliance controls;

(f) confirm the make-up of the board and demonstrate the independence of the non-executive directors; and

(g) splitting the role of chairman and chief executive.

8.5   Directors' remuneration

The directors' report to its shareholders in the annual report and accounts will need to specify:

(a) the company's policy on executive directors' remuneration;

(b) a breakdown of each director's remuneration package for the relevant period including basic salary and any fees, the estimated value of benefits in kind, annual bonuses, deferred bonuses, compensation which is payable if any directors lose their position as directors, any payments for breach of contract by the company, and any other payments payable on termination;

(c) each director's share options;

(d) details of any long-term incentive plans – identifying any director's interests and any cash payments or other benefits received by each director as well as a statement of the company's policy on granting options or awards;

(e) details of any director's service contract with a notice period in excess of one year, giving reasons for such notice period; and

(f) full details of each director's pension entitlement and the amount of any increase in value of a director's pension fund (or the benefits thereunder) and its transfer value.

The Hampel Committee suggested (as mentioned earlier) that boards should aim to reduce the notice periods in directors' service contracts to one year or less, although recognising that this is not likely to be achieved immediately. Whilst it agreed with Cadbury in saying that non-executive directors should not participate in share option schemes, it had no objection to the payment of non-executive directors in shares. The Hampel Committee also considered that there was some advantage in including a provision in the director's service contract at the outset for a payment to be made to the director if he is removed from office, except for misconduct. The Committee suggested that dealing with what a director would be entitled to, if fairly dismissed in his service contract, would enable shareholders to be aware of the entitlement so removing any suggestion that the issue (if it arises) is unclear and that they were not previously aware of such a provision.

In March 2001, Stephen Buyers, the Secretary of State for Trade and Industry, announced some proposed changes to the disclosure requirements for directors' remuneration which may be included in the next Companies Act. This follows on from the DTI consultation paper on directors' remuneration entitled "*Paying for Performance: The New Framework for Executive Remuneration*".

The proposals will require all the company's to disclose details of the directors remuneration in a single report which will then in turn become an integral part of the company's annual reporting cycle. The report will need to contain the following pieces of information:

(a) *board consideration of remuneration* – details of the remuneration committee, the name of any firms retained as "remuneration consultants" and whether the board accepted the remuneration committee's recommendation;

(b) *statement of policy on directors' pay* – including details of the performance criteria, share options and long term incentives. Also including details of comparable companies and details of the company's policy on service contracts and notice periods for executive directors;

(c) *details of each directors remuneration in the preceding financial year;*

(d) *performance graphs* – to provide historic information on the company's performance, showing comparisons with other companies in the same sector and market indices. This requirement is to be modelled on the US Securities and Exchange Commission graph.

Details of the consultation document can be found at www.dti.gov.uk/cld/promdocs.htm. It is proposed that these requirements be inserted to the amendment to the Companies Act 1985.

8.6 The re-election of directors

The directors of a PLC will have to offer themselves for re-election at regular intervals (typically every three years). Companies that do not as yet conform to this principle should, as proposed, make the necessary changes to their articles of association as soon as possible.

The Hampel Committee recommended that all the names of directors submitted for election or re-election should be accompanied with biographies indicating their relevant qualifications and experience.

Ideally, a third of the Board of Directors should be non-executive and the roles of chairman and chief executive should be split.

All directors should receive appropriate training on taking up their first appointment to the board of a listed company and should receive further training as necessary, particularly on relevant new rules and regulations, and changing commercial rights.

Independent non-executive directors should constitute a "Remuneration Committee" and a majority should sit on an "Audit Committee".

The directors are encouraged to organise presentations to shareholders at AGMs.

Directors should have the right to seek independent advice (at the company's cost) on key issues.

8.7 Shareholders

The Hampel Committee strongly recommended that institutional shareholders, wherever practicable, vote all the shares under their control. It also recommended that companies should announce their total proxy votes for, and against, each resolution once it had been dealt with at the meeting on a show of hands, in the hope that this will encourage higher levels of voting by the institutions.

It was recommended that a resolution should be proposed at the company's AGM to approve its report and accounts, and that notices to shareholders should be circulated at least 20 working days in advance of that meeting. It was also suggested that shareholders should be able to vote on each substantially separate issue to ensure that the practice of "bundling" unrelated proposals into a single resolution ceases.

8.8   Conclusion

In the future, directors will be much more accountable to their shareholders – both in terms of their behaviour and their company's behaviour, but also as to how they are to be remunerated. AIM company directors need to be aware of this trend, especially if a significant percentage of the company's shares are held by institutions.

MODEL DOCUMENTATION

Tom Mackay
Partner – Head of ABC Corporate
Amhurst Brown Colombotti

With thanks to Deloitte & Touche for their contribution to Appendix 1

APPENDIX 1
AIM ADMISSION DOCUMENT

THIS DOCUMENT IS IMPORTANT AND REQUIRES YOUR IMMEDIATE ACTION. If you are in any doubt about the contents of this document you should consult a person authorised under the Financial Services and Markets Act 2000 who specialises in advising on the acquisition of shares and other securities.[1]

This document has been drawn up in accordance with the Public Offers of Securities Regulations 1995 ("POS Regulations").[2] A copy of this document has been delivered to the Registrar of Companies in England and Wales for registration in accordance with regulation 4 (2) of the POS Regulations.[3]

The Directors (whose names and business addresses appear in section 1.2 part one of this document) declare that to the best of their knowledge the information contained in this document is in accordance with the facts and that the document makes no omission likely to affect the import of such information.[4] All the Directors accept responsibility for this document.[5]

The Alternative Investment Market (AIM) is a market designed primarily for emerging or smaller companies to which a higher investment risk tends to be attached than to larger or more established companies. AIM securities are not Officially Listed. A prospective investor should be aware of the risks of investing in such companies and should make the decision to invest only after careful consideration and if appropriate, consultation with an independent financial adviser. London Stock Exchange plc has not itself examined or approved the contents of the document.[6]

[COMPANY NAME][7]
(incorporated and registered in England and Wales, registered number •)

**Offer for Subscription of up to • Ordinary Shares of
• each at a price of • per share**

Nominated Adviser: [Nominated Adviser][8]

---

[1] Required by POS Reg. Sch. 1, para. 8.
[2] Required by POS Reg. Sch. 1, para. 7.
[3] Required by POS Reg. Sch. 1, para. 6.
[4] Required by POS Reg. Sch. 1, para. 10(1).
[5] Required by POS Reg. Sch. 1, para 10(2).
[6] Required by AIM Rule Sch. 2(d). See also POS Reg. Sch. 1, para. 16.
[7] POS Reg. Sch. 1, paras 2 and 3 require the name of the issuer and if different the name of the person offering the securities.
[8] The name of the nominated adviser must be on the first page, prominently and in bold. AIM Rule Sch. 2(d).

Share Capital

Authorised			Issued and fully paid[9] (assuming the Offer is subscribed in full)	
Number	Amount		Number	Amount
•	•	Ordinary Shares of •p each•	•	•

[Nominated Adviser], which is regulated by The Securities and Futures Authority Limited, is acting as the Company's nominated advisor and nominated broker in connection with the Admission. Its responsibilities as the Company's nominated adviser under the AIM Rules are owed solely to London Stock Exchange plc and are not owed to the Company or to any Director or to any other person in respect of his decision to acquire shares in the Company in reliance on any part of this document. No representation or warranty, express or implied, is made by [Nominated Adviser] as to any of the contents of this document (without limiting the statutory rights of any person to whom this document is issued). [Nominated Adviser] will not be offering advice and will not otherwise be responsible for providing customer protections to recipients of this document in respect of the Offer or any acquisition of shares in the Company.

At the close of business on •, the Group had a bank overdraft of •, a bank loan of •, a factoring balance of •, and outstanding hire purchase commitments of •. Save as aforesaid, at the close of business on •, no member of the Group had any loan capital (including term loans) issued, or created but unissued, or any borrowings or indebtedness in the nature of borrowings, including bank overdrafts, liabilities under acceptances (other than normal trade bills), acceptance credits, hire purchase commitments, obligations under finance leases, guarantees or other contingent liabilities. At the close of business on •, the Group had cash and bank balances of £•.[10]

---

[9] POS Reg. Sch.1, para 35 requires the amount of the issuer's issued share capital.
[10] An indebtedness statement is not required by the POS Regs or by the AIM Rules but is often inserted.

Appendix 1 – AIM Admission Document

CONTENTS

		Section
PART ONE	DEFINITIONS	1.1
	DIRECTORS AND ADVISERS	1.2
	KEY INFORMATION	1.3
PART TWO	INFORMATION ON THE GROUP	
	Industry background	2.1
	Description of the Company and its business activities	2.2
	Directors and senior management	2.3
	Participation in the Offer for Subscription	2.4
	Reasons for the offer and use of proceeds	2.5
	Marketability of Ordinary Shares	2.6
	Dividend policy	2.7
	Corporate governance	2.8
	CREST	2.9
	Risk factors	2.10
	Tax considerations	2.11
PART THREE	FINANCIAL INFORMATION ON THE GROUP	
PART FOUR	ILLUSTRATIVE PROJECTIONS	
PART FIVE	ADDITIONAL INFORMATION	

A Practitioner's Guide to the Alternative Investment Market Rules

PART SIX   TERMS AND CONDITIONS OF APPLICATION

How to complete the Application Form

Application Form

Appendix 1 – AIM Admission Document

PART ONE
SECTION 1.1 DEFINITIONS

The following definitions apply throughout this document, unless the context requires otherwise:-

"Admission"	admission of all the issued Ordinary Shares (including the New Ordinary Shares) to AIM
"AIM"	the Alternative Investment Market operated by London Stock Exchange plc
"Application Form"	the application form at the rear of this document
"Board" or "Directors"	the board of directors of the Company
"Company"	[Company Name]
"Group"	the Company and its subsidiary undertakings
"Minimum Amount"	£•
"New Ordinary Shares"	up to • Ordinary Shares to be issued pursuant to the Offer for Subscription
"Nominated Adviser"	[Nominated Adviser]
"Official List"	the official list of the United Kingdom Listing Authority
"Ordinary Shares"	ordinary shares of •p each in the capital of the Company
"Offer for Subscription" or "Offer"	the offer for subscription of • Ordinary Shares in accordance with this document
"Offer Price"	•p per Ordinary Share
"POS Regulations"	Public Offers of Securities Regulations 1995, as amended
"Receiving Agent"	•

A Practitioner's Guide to the Alternative Investment Market Rules

"Share Option Scheme" the share option scheme adopted by the Company, further details of which are set out in paragraph •, PART • of this document

"Subsidiary" [Subsidiary]

Appendix 1 – AIM Admission Document

SECTION 1.2 DIRECTORS & ADVISERS

Directors[11]

Chairman

Managing director

Finance director

Non-executive

[address of directors][12]

Secretary

Registered office[13]

Nominated adviser

[Nominated broker]

[Broker]

Solicitors to the Company [and the Offer]

Solicitors to the Offer

Auditors [and reporting accountants][14]

Registrars [and receiving agents]

---

[11] POS Reg. Sch. 1, para. 4 requires "the names and functions of the directors ...".
[12] POS Reg. Sch.1, para 9 requires "the names, addresses (home or business) and functions of those persons responsible ... for the prospectus or any part of the prospectus, specifying such part".
[13] POS Reg. Sch. 1, paras 2 and 3 requires the address of the issuer's registered office and if different the address of the person offering the securities.
[14] Reporting accountants are not necessary. The POS Regs require either the actual audited accounts or an accountant's report.

125

A Practitioner's Guide to the Alternative Investment Market Rules

SECTION 1.3 KEY INFORMATION

The following information should be read in conjunction with the full text of this document, from which it is derived.[15] You should read the whole of this document and not just rely on the key information set out below. **In particular, your attention is drawn to the principal risk factors, set out in Section • of this document.**

Offer statistics

Up to • ordinary shares[16] will be issued pursuant to the Offer for Subscription to raise a minimum of £• and a maximum of £• before expenses.

The following statistics are based on the assumption that the Offer is subscribed in full.

Offer Price[17]	•p
Market capitalisation at the Offer Price	£• million
Ordinary Shares in issue immediately following the Offer	•
Percentage of enlarged issued share capital subject to the Offer	•%
Expected total proceeds of the Offer	£•
Expected net proceeds of the Offer after expenses[18]	£•

---

[15] The key information should be completed and derived from Part Two when Part Two is substantially complete/verified.
[16] POS Reg Sch. 1, para 18 requires "The number of securities being issued" and para 19 "The number of securities being offered".
[17] POS Reg Sch. 1, para 26 requires "The price at which the securities are offered or, if appropriate, the procedure, method and timetable for their delivery".
[18] POS Reg Sch. 1, para 20 requires "The total proceeds which it is expected will be raised by the offer and the expected net proceeds, after deduction of the expenses, of the offer".

Appendix 1 – AIM Admission Document

Timetable of principal events	
Publication of Prospectus	•
Opening[19] of subscription list	•
Latest time and date[20] for receipt of Application forms (unless extended)	• am/pm
CREST accounts credited	•
Expected date of despatch of share certificates (where applicable)	•
Expected date of Admission and date of first dealing	• am/pm

---

[19] Three days after publication.
[20] Maximum of 40 days after publication. Also POS Reg Sch. 1 para 2 requires "The period during which the offer of the securities is open".

A Practitioner's Guide to the Alternative Investment Market Rules

PART TWO
INFORMATION ON THE GROUP

Section 2.1
　　Industry background

Section 2.2
　　Description[21] of the Company and its business activities[22]

Section 2.3
　　Directors and senior management[23]

Section 2.4
　　Participation in the Offer for Subscription

Up to • Ordinary Shares are being offered for subscription at •p per share, to raise £• before expenses and approximately £• after expenses (excluding VAT).[24] If only the Minimum Amount is received the Offer will raise approximately £• after expenses.

The Offer, which is not underwritten, is conditional [upon the Company's application to join AIM being accepted and] upon valid applications being received for the Minimum Amount. If the condition[s] of the Offer [is] [are] not satisfied the Offer for Subscription will lapse and any monies received from

---

[21] POS Reg. 9 states that in addition to the specific information requirements a prospectus shall:
　"(1)　... contain all such information as investors would reasonably require, and reasonably expect to find there, for the purpose of making an informed assessment of:
　　(a)　the assets and liabilities, financial position, profits and losses, and prospects of the issuer of the securities; and
　　(b)　the rights attaching to those securities.
　(2)　The information to be included by the virtue of this regulation shall be such information as is mentioned in paragraph (1) which is within the knowledge of any person responsible for the prospectus or which it would be reasonable for him to obtain by making enquiries.
　(3)　In determining what information is require to be included in a prospectus by virtue of this regulation regard shall be had to the nature of the securities and of the issuer of the securities."

[22] POS Reg. Sch. 1, para. 41, 42, 43, 48 and 49 requires:
　(i)　a description of the issuer's principal activities and of any exceptional factors which have influenced its activities;
　(ii)　a statement of any dependence of the issuer on patents or other intellectual property rights, licences or particular contracts, where any of these are of fundamental importance to the issuer's business;
　(iii)　information regarding investments in progress where they are significant;
　(iv)　the significant recent trends concerning the development of the issuer's business since the end of the last completed financial year of the issuer;
　(v)　information on the issuer's prospects for at least the current financial year of the issuer.

[23] AIM Rule Sch. 2(f)(i) requires "the director's full name, any previous names and age". This also applies to each proposed director.

[24] POS Reg. Sch. 1, para. 18, 19 and 20 requires "The number of securities being offered" and "The total proceeds which it is expected will be raised by the offer and the expected net proceeds, after deduction of the expenses, of the offer."

Appendix 1 – AIM Admission Document

applicants will be returned to them by first class post at the risk of the applicant, within seven days of the closing date of the Offer. Applications must be made on the Application Form (a copy of which is at the rear of this document). Details of the terms and conditions of application and the procedure for application are set out in PART [SIX] of this document. The Directors reserve the right to reject in whole or in part or to scale down any application.

The subscription list will open at •am on • and may be closed at any time thereafter, but no later than •pm on •[unless extended by the Directors].[25] The subscription price of •p per share is payable in full on application; share certificates[26] for successful applicants and any surplus application monies will be sent at the risk of the addressee to those persons entitled by post within • days of the Offer becoming unconditional [or, in respect of cleared funds received after the Offer becomes unconditional, within • days of receipt of such cleared funds]. In the case of applicants requesting shares in uncertificated form, it is expected that the appropriate CREST stock amounts of successful applicants will be credited with effect from • where appropriate.

The Ordinary Shares will, following allotment, rank pari passu in all respects with the existing issued Ordinary Shares and will have the right to receive all dividends and other distributions hereafter declared or made in respect of the issued ordinary share capital of the Company.

Section 2.5
Reasons for the Offer and use of proceeds[27]

[The net proceeds available to the Company after the expenses of the Offer are expected to amount to approximately £• million. These proceeds will provide additional working capital ...]

The Directors believe that admission to AIM will help raise the profile of the Company as well as helping it to attract and retain key employees whom the Company will be able to incentivise through share schemes. In addition, it is expected that Admission will provide the Company with potential access to further capital the opportunity to make acquisitions, should suitable opportunities arise, through *inter alia*, the issue of shares.

---

[25] POS Reg.Sch 1 para. 25 requires "The period during which the offer of the securities is open."
[26] POS Reg. Sch. 1, para. 27 requires "The arrangements for payment for the securities being offered and the arrangements and timetable for their delivery".
[27] POS Reg. Sch. 1, para. 17 "The purpose for which the securities are being issued".

Section 2.6
Lock in and orderly marketing arrangements

Each of the Directors, has, under the terms of the Placing Agreement, agreed that for the period from the date of Admission up to and including the date of publication of the results of the Company for the period ending •, he will not (and will procure in so far as he is able that any person with whom he is connected for the purposes of section 346 of the Act will not), save in certain specified circumstances dispose of any Ordinary Shares held by him on Admission. The circumstances in which disposals will be allowed include a sale of shares with the prior written consent of [Broker] and the Board, (with the Director wishing to make the disposal being excluded from participating in such decision); disposals by way of gift to family members to trusts for family members or to charitable trusts; disposals pursuant to a general offer for the share capital of the Company; disposals pursuant to a scheme of arrangement or reconstruction; disposals on death or cessation of employment; or disposal on a purchase by the Company of its own shares. Any disposals by the Directors permitted during this period must be made through [Broker] (save for disposals by way of gift set out above).

Section 2.7
Corporate Governance

The Directors intend to comply with the Combined Code on the Principles of Good Governance and Code of Best Practice in such respects as are appropriate for a company of its size and nature. An audit committee and a remuneration committee (each comprising a majority of non-executive directors) have been established [to operate with effect from Admission].

The audit committee will meet at least twice each year. The audit committee will be responsible for ensuring that the financial performance of the Group is properly monitored and reported on. It will have the opportunity to meet the auditors without executive Board members being present and will review reports relating to accounts and internal control systems.

The remuneration committee will review the performance of executive directors and set their remuneration. The remuneration committee will also make recommendations to the full Board concerning remuneration and the allocation of share options to directors and employees. The remuneration and terms of appointment of non-executive directors will be set by the Board.

Appendix 1 – AIM Admission Document

Section 2.8
Dividend policy

[The payment of dividends will be subject to the availability of distributable reserves whilst maintaining an appropriate level of dividend cover and having regard to the need to retain sufficient funds to finance the developments of the Group's activities. The Directors' current intention is to re-invest funds directly into the Company rather than to fund the payment of dividends, for at least until the end of the first full financial year following the Offer. The Board will continue to review its dividend policy as the Group develops.]

Section 2.9
Crest

CREST is a paperless settlement procedure enabling securities to be evidenced otherwise than by certificate and transferred otherwise than by written instrument. Application [has been made] [will be made] for the Ordinary Shares to be admitted to CREST. It is expected that the Ordinary Shares will be enabled for settlement in, and admitted to CREST [on the date that admission of the Ordinary Shares to AIM becomes effective] [as soon as practicable after Admission has become effective].

Section 2.10
Risk factors

Investors should be aware of the risks associated with an investment in the Company. In particular, the following risk factors should be considered:

- The value of the Ordinary Shares may go down as well as up. Investors may therefore realise less than their original investment.

- [It may be necessary for the Company to raise additional capital to enable the Group to progress through further stages of development.]

- [The development of the Company's business is at an early stage and the growth of sales may not happen as rapidly as the Directors anticipate.]

- [If only the Minimum Amount is raised, the growth of sales may be slower than projected.]

- [The Group has a small management team and the loss of a key individual could affect the Group's business.]

An investment in the Company may not be suitable for all recipients of this document. Potential investors are accordingly advised to consult a person authorised under the Financial Services Act 1986 who specialises in advising in investments of this kind before making any investment decisions.

Section 2.11
United Kingdom Taxation considerations[28]

Your attention is drawn to paragraph • in Part • of this document where information relevant to a potential investor's tax position is set out. The following statements are intended only as a general guide to current United Kingdom tax legislation and to what is understood to be the current practice of the United Kingdom Inland Revenue (the "Inland Revenue") and may not apply to certain classes of shareholder (such as dealers in securities). Any person who is in any doubt as to his tax position is strongly recommended to consult his professional advisers immediately.[but certain current potential tax benefits are summarised below in respect of an individual resident in the UK for tax purposes.]

[On issue, the Ordinary Shares will not be treated as either "listed" or "quoted" securities for UK tax purposes. Provided that the Company remains a company which does not have any of its shares quoted on a recognised stock exchange (which for these purposes does not include having its shares admitted to trading on AIM) and assuming that the Company remains a trading company or the holding company of a trading group for UK tax purposes, the Ordinary Shares should continue to be treated as unquoted securities for UK tax purposes.]

Inheritance tax ("IHT") business property relief

[Individuals subscribing for Ordinary Shares may be entitled to IHT business property relief (Chapter 1 of Part V of the Inheritance Tax Act 1984). Subject to fulfilling the relevant conditions for relief, an individual will be eligible for the 100% exemption from IHT for unquoted shares (which includes AIM securities) such as the Ordinary Shares. There is a minimum period of ownership for relief to apply and additional conditions for transfers within seven years before an investor's death. Broadly, if an investor makes a lifetime gift of his Ordinary Shares or dies while a holder of those shares, then no IHT should be payable provided that the investor held the Ordinary Shares for two years prior to the date

---

[28] This section while perhaps helpful to the investor is not required by the law and should only be inserted if checked by a tax adviser. The law only requires "Particulars of tax on income from the securities withheld at source, including tax credits" (POS Reg. Sch.1, para.13). This is dealt with in para. 12 Part Five.

Appendix 1 – AIM Admission Document

of the transfer or death. The Company does not undertake to conduct its activities in a way designed to preserve any IHT business property relief claimed by investors.]

CGT holdover relief

[Individuals subscribing for Ordinary Shares may be eligible for CGT holdover relief on certain disposals (other than to a company) of Ordinary Shares otherwise than at arm's length (for example, by gift). On issue the date of issue, [the company will be a trading company or the holding company of a trading group and therefore,] the Ordinary Shares should be treated as business assets for the purpose of CGT holdover relief. This relief is given by way of "holdover" of the gains otherwise chargeable, i.e. the CGT liability is postponed until the individual to whom the Ordinary Shares have been transferred subsequently makes a chargeable disposal and his base cost is taken to be the transferor's CGT base cost. The relief must be claimed within six years of the end of the relevant tax year by both the transferor and the transferee. The Company does not undertake to conduct its activities in a way designed to preserve any holdover relief claimed by investors.]

Enterprise investment scheme ("EIS")

[The Company is seeking provisional confirmation from the Inland Revenue that it will qualify under the terms of the EIS. It will apply for formal approval once the shares are issued or the company has commenced to trade. The time limit for this application is the later of two years, from the time when the shares are issued, or the end of four months after the trade has commenced.]

[Individuals may be able to deduct an amount equal to tax at the lower [20%] rate on the amount subscribed for fully paid Ordinary Shares from their total liability to income tax for the current year. A claim can also be made for part of the relief to be related to the preceding tax year. An individual investor must not be connected with the Company in order to obtain the relief (or become connected with it within the next three years if he is to retain relief). It does not matter where the individual is resident for tax purposes.]

[Claims for relief must be made not later than five years after the time limit for filing the relevant year's self assessment return. In order to obtain the relief each investor must submit a claim to his Tax District together with a tax certificate from the Company. An individual cannot claim relief in respect of any amount subscribed for Ordinary Shares in excess of £150,000 in any tax year. The spouse of a claimant is also entitled to claim relief on his/her own investments.]

[Relief will be clawed back if the company ceases to carry on a qualifying trade within three years or the funds raised are not used for the qualifying trade within 12 months of the date of the share issue or the commencement of the trade.]

[Relief will be restricted or withdrawn if the claimant receives value (other than dividend) from the Company (or a person connected with the Company) during the five-year period beginning two years before issue of the shares or disposes of the shares within three years of their date of issue. Relief will also be restricted or withdrawn where certain arrangements, including a guaranteed exit scheme, existed before or at the time of issue of the shares. If EIS relief is given at the lower rate of income tax and is not withdrawn, any gain accruing to an individual on the first disposal three or more years after the issue of EIS shares is not chargeable to capital gains tax. Where EIS relief is not given on the full amount subscribed for the shares (other than by reason of the income tax liability being insufficient to support the relief) the capital gains tax exemption is restricted to a proportion of the gain only. Where the same circumstances apply but a loss is incurred on the first disposal, in calculating the loss, the original amount subscribed by the individual is treated as reduced by the amount of the EIS relief given and not withdrawn. The resulting loss can be set against gains or taxable income in the year in which the disposal occurs.]

Capital Gains Tax ("CGT") deferral relief

Capital gains deferral relief is available for reinvestment into shares on which EIS income tax relief is claimed. It is no longer a requirement that the shares qualify for income tax relief nor that the individual be unconnected with the Company. Furthermore, there is no limit on the amount of gain that may be deferred so that the income tax maximum relief of £150,000 no longer applies. However, deferral relief will only be available to an individual resident in the UK (for tax purposes) who subscribes wholly in cash for eligible shares in an EIS company which are issued within one year immediately preceding or three years immediately following the time the capital gain in question accrues.

[The deferred capital gain will be re-instated for the tax year when you dispose (other than to a spouse) of the new shares. The capital gain will also be revived if the conditions for the relief relating to the Company cease to be satisfied or you cease to be UK tax resident during the period of three years beginning with the date of issue of the shares. Relief will also be wholly or partly withdrawn if the claimant receives value (other than dividend) from the Company.]

Appendix 1 – AIM Admission Document

Capital Gains Taper relief

For Capital Gains Tax purposes of individuals Taper relief now applies and operates by reducing the amount of gain chargeable by a percentage amount that is dependent on the period of ownership, and the status of the company as an "unlisted" trading company [or holding company of a trading group]. On the assumption that the shares are business assets the higher percentage of taper relief will apply so that after more than four years of ownership it is 75%. [June 2001 - Chancellor statement states this maximum relief applies after just two years of ownership.] The company cannot guarantee that at all times the shares will be regarded by the Inland Revenue as business assets.

The above is a summary of the general nature of certain reliefs which may be available and should not be construed as constituting advice. Further information on taxation is set out in paragraph • of PART FIVE of this document. A potential investor should obtain his own advice from their own investment or taxation adviser before applying for any Ordinary Shares.

A Practitioner's Guide to the Alternative Investment Market Rules

PART THREE
FINANCIAL INFORMATION[29] ON THE GROUP

The Directors
[Company Name]

The Directors
[Nominated Adviser]

Ladies and Gentlemen,

We report that [Company Name] ("the Company") was incorporated in England on • as a public limited company with company number •. We have acted as auditors to the Company since its incorporation.

The Company has not commenced to trade and therefore no profit or loss has occurred. No audited financial statements have been prepared in respect of any period since incorporation. No transactions have occurred other than:

(a)   The issue of two ordinary shares of • pence each and the issue of • ordinary shares of • pence each credited as fully paid in consideration of the transfer to the company on • of the entire issued share capital of [Subsidiary];

(b)   The entry into the material contracts referred to in paragraph • of Part • of the prospectus relating to the offer for subscription to be issued by the Company on • ("the prospectus");and

(c)   No dividend has been declared or paid.

In our opinion, the above report gives a true and fair view of the state of affairs and of the profit or loss of the Company and we consent to the inclusion of this report in the prospectus in the form and context in which it appears and accept responsibility for it accordingly.

Yours faithfully

[Auditor]

---

[29] POS Reg. Sch. 1, para. 45 contains the accounting information required. This gives the option of inserting either the accounts or a report on the Group for the last three years or if shorter for the financial years during its existence (disregarding a financial year which ends less than three months before the date on which the offer is first made and for which accounts have been prepared by that date). There are requirements for interim accounts or a report if the date of the offer is more than nine months since the financial year end.

Appendix 1 – AIM Admission Document

The Directors
[Company Name]

The Directors

Ladies and Gentlemen,

As auditors of [Company name] [Subsidiary], we consent to the inclusion of our accountants' report on [Company Name] [Subsidiary] for the period ended • and our audit reports on [Company name] [Subsidiary] in respect of the accounts for the years ending • and • in the prospectus relating to the offer for subscription of • shares in [Company Name] dated •. We confirm that we accept responsibility for the audit reports and have not become aware, since the date of the reports, of any matters affecting the validity of the audit reports.

Yours faithfully

[AUDITOR]

PART FOUR
ILLUSTRATIVE PROJECTIONS[30]

The Directors
[Company Name]

The Directors

Ladies and Gentlemen,

We have reviewed the accounting policies and calculations used in the preparation of the Illustrative Projections of [Company Name] and its wholly owned subsidiary [Subsidiary] (together "the Group"), for the two years ending •, as set out in Part • of the Company's Prospectus dated • ("the Prospectus").

The Illustrative Projections, for which the directors of the Company are solely responsible, are based upon assumptions made by the directors which cannot be confirmed and verified in the same way as historical results. The principal assumptions are summarised in Part • of the Prospectus.

It should be appreciated that the Group's projections have been prepared for the purposes of illustration and do not constitute a forecast. Because the projections cover a period of trading based on agreements which are not yet in place, the assumptions are necessarily more subjective than would be appropriate for a forecast. Events and circumstances frequently do not occur as expected and the actual results may therefore differ materially from those projected.

We draw your attention, in particular, to the section headed "Risk factors" set out in Part • of the Prospectus, which describes the directors' views of the principal risks associated with a business to which the projections relate. For these reasons, we do not express any opinion either on the validity of the assumptions or the possibility of the projected results being achieved.

---

[30] The larger accountancy firms are now reluctant to give opinions on illustrative projections.

Appendix 1 – AIM Admission Document

In our opinion, the Illustrative Projections, [so far as the accounting policies and calculations are concerned], have been properly compiled on the basis of the directors' assumptions and are presented on a basis consistent with the accounting policies normally adopted by the Group.

Yours faithfully

[AUDITOR]

A Practitioner's Guide to the Alternative Investment Market Rules

Illustrative Projections[31]

The Directors have carefully examined the Group's prospects and, on the basis of the principal assumptions set out below, they have prepared the following illustrative projections for the two year period ending •. These have been based on the directors' perception of the market place and illustrate the potential level of profitability should their estimates prove to be correct. The directors state that the illustrative projections have been made after due and careful enquiry and the Nominated Adviser has confirmed to the Company that it has satisfied itself that the illustrative projections have been made after due and careful enquiry by the Directors. Nevertheless, there is no guarantee that they will be achieved.

The illustrative projections set out below are not, and are not intended to be, forecasts and should not be relied upon as forecasts by the investors. Results actually achieved are likely to differ significantly from the projections. Attention is drawn to the risk factors set out in Part • section • of this document which should be carefully considered in conjunction with these projections.

Profit and loss account

	Year Ending • £000's	Year Ending • £000's
Turnover		
Cost of sales		
Gross profit		
Overheads		
Operating profit		
Interest receivable		
Interest payable and similar charges		
Profit on ordinary activities before taxation		
Taxation		
Profit on ordinary activities after taxation		

---

[31] Where the AIM Admission Document contains a profit forecast, estimate or projection (which includes any form of words which expressly or by implication states a minimum or maximum for the likely level of profits or losses for a period subsequent to that for which audited accounts have been published, or contains data from which a calculation of an approximate figure for future profits or losses may be made, even if no particular figure is mentioned and the words "profit" or "loss" are not used) the documents must disclosed:
   (i)   a statement by its directors that such forecast, estimate or projection has been made after due and careful enquiry by the issuer;
   (ii)   a statement of the principal assumptions for each factor which could have a material effect on the achievement of the forecast, estimate or projection. The assumptions must be readily understandable by investors and be specific and precise; and
   (iii) confirmation from the nominated adviser to the applicant that it has satisfied itself that the forecast, estimate or projection has been made after due and careful enquiry by the directors of the applicant. (AIM Rule Sch 2(c))

Appendix 1 – AIM Admission Document

Principal assumptions

The following principal assumptions have been used by the Directors in preparing the illustrative projections shown above, which have been prepared applying the historical cost convention.

- [It is assumed that the existing customer base will continue to trade with the Group, with similar turnover levels as historically experienced.]
- [Additional turnover will be achieved from new customers based on the directors' views of agreements currently in negotiation.]
- [It is assumed that the offer is fully subscribed.]
- [No account has been taken of any dividend payments.]
- [It is assumed that there is no inflation.]

A Practitioner's Guide to the Alternative Investment Market Rules

PART FIVE
ADDITIONAL INFORMATION

1. **The Company**

    The Company was incorporated in England and Wales[32] on • as a public limited company[33] under the Companies Act 1985 (the "Act"), registered[34] with number • and with the name [company name].[35] The liability of the members of the Company is limited.[36]

    The Company's principal place of business in the United Kingdom is at •.[37]

2. **Share Capital**

    2.1   On the date of this document, the authorised share capital[38] of the Company was £• divided into • ordinary shares of £• each of which • such shares were issued and are fully paid.[39]

    2.2   On • by resolution passed at an extraordinary general meeting of the Company it was resolved that:

    (a)   the Directors were generally and unconditionally authorised, pursuant to section 80 of the Act to allot relevant securities (as defined in that section) up to a maximum nominal amount equal to the nominal amount of the authorised but unissued share capital at the date of the passing of the resolution, such authority to expire at the commencement of the annual general meeting of the Company next following the date upon which such resolution was passed except as regards an allotment being made thereafter pursuant to an offer or agreement made by the Company before such date;

---

[32]   POS Reg. Sch.1 para.29 requires "The date and place of incorporation of the issuer ..."
[33]   POS Reg. 31 requires "The legal form of the issuer, the legislation under which it was formed ..."
[34]   POS Reg 30 requires "The place of registration of the issuer and the number with which it is registered."
[35]   POS Reg. Sch. 1, para. 2 requires "The name of the issuer and the address of its registered office." See also POS Reg. Sch. 1, para. 29, 30 and 31.
[36]   POS Reg. Sch. 1, para. 33 states "If the liability of the members of the issuer is limited, a statement of that fact."
[37]   POS Reg para 29 requires "... In the case of an issuer not incorporated in the United Kingdom, the address of its principal place of business in the United Kingdom (if any)."
[38]   POS Reg. Sch. 1, para. 34 requires "The amount of the issuer's authorised share capital and any limit on the duration of the authorisation to issue such share capital."
[39]   POS Reg. Sch.1, para. 37 requires "The number of shares of each class making up each of the authorised and issued share capital, the nominal value of such shares and in the case of the issued share capital, the amount paid up on the shares. See also POS Reg Sch. 1, para. 35.

Appendix 1 – AIM Admission Document

(b) pursuant to section 95 of the Act the rights of pre-emption[40] in respect of Ordinary Shares be disapplied such disapplication to expire at the commencement of the annual general meeting of the Company next following the date upon which such resolution was passed except as regards an allotment being made thereafter pursuant to an offer or agreement made by the Company before such date such power being limited to the allotment of:

   (i) up to • Ordinary Shares for the share for share agreement referred to at paragraph •;

   (ii) up to • Ordinary Shares for the Offer for Subscription;

   (iii) up to • Ordinary Shares (being equivalent to • percent of the issued Ordinary Shares after the Offer for Subscription assuming full subscription) for the Company's Share Option Scheme;

   (iv) up to • Ordinary Shares (being equivalent to • percent. of the issued Ordinary Shares after the Offer for Subscription assuming full subscription) for the options referred to at paragraph •; and

   (v) up to • Ordinary Shares (being equivalent to • percent. of the issued Ordinary Shares after the Offer for Subscription assuming full subscription) for cash otherwise than pursuant to (i) through (iv) of this sub-paragraph •;

(c) a draft agreement relating to the purchase by the Company of the entire issued share capital of [Subsidiary] be approved;

(d) the rules constituting the Share Option Scheme be approved;

(e) the Directors be authorised to grant the options referred to at paragraph •;

2.3 By an agreement dated • between the Company and all the shareholders of [Subsidiary] the Company acquired the whole issued share capital of [Subsidiary], the consideration for which was satisfied by the allotment and issue of • Ordinary Shares (which includes the two subscribers shares) credited as fully paid, which represents the total issued share capital of the Company prior to the Offer for Subscription.

---

[40] POS Reg. Sch. 1, para 14 requires "The procedure for the exercise of any right of pre-emption attaching to the securities."

2.4 By an agreement dated • the Company granted an option to • in respect of up to • Ordinary Shares at a price per share of £•. The option must be exercised before •.[41]

2.5 Save as disclosed in the foregoing sub-paragraphs of this paragraph 2 and paragraph 3 below (which relates to the Company's subsidiary, [Subsidiary]):

(a) no share or loan capital of the Company, or of any other company within the Group, is under option or has been agreed, conditionally or unconditionally, to be put under option;

(b) other than for the Offer or upon the exercise of options duly granted pursuant to the Share Option Scheme or upon a due exercise of the options referred to in paragraph 2.4 above, there is no present intention to issue any of the authorised but unissued share capital of the Company.

2.6 The Ordinary Shares are in registered form. It is expected that share certificates will be posted within • days of the Minimum Amount being raised in cleared funds, or in respect of cleared funds received after the Offer becomes unconditional within • days of receipt of such cleared funds. No temporary documents of title will be issued.

3. **Subsidiaries**[42]

3.1 The Company's only subsidiary is [Subsidiary], which is a wholly-owned subsidiary and is the main trading company of the Group.

3.2 [Subsidiary] was incorporated in England and Wales on • with registered number • under the Act as a private company limited by shares. The registered office is at •.

3.3 The authorised share capital of [Subsidiary] on incorporation was £• divided into • ordinary shares of £• each, of which two subscriber shares were issued [fully paid for cash at par].

3.4 On • the authorised share capital of [Subsidiary] was increased from £• to £• by the creation of • ordinary shares of £• each.

3.5 Between • and • • ordinary shares were issued in [Subsidiary] for cash.

---

[41] POS Reg. Sch. 1, para 38 requires "The amount of any outstanding listed and unlisted securities issued by the issuer, the conditions and procedures for their conversion and the number of shares which would be issued as a result of their conversion."
[42] POS Reg. Sch. 1, para. 39 requires "If the issuer is a member of a group, a brief description of the group and of the issuer's position in it, stating, where the issuer is a subsidiary, the name of its holding company."

Appendix 1 – AIM Admission Document

3.6   On • all the issued share capital in [Subsidiary] was acquired by the Company.

4. **Memorandum of Association**[43]

   The memorandum of association of the Company provides that the Company's principal object is to act as a general commercial company. The objects of the Company are set out in full in clause 4 of the Memorandum of Association of the Company.

5. **Articles of Association**[44]

   The articles of association of the Company (the "Articles") include provisions to the following effect:

5.1   *Votes of members*

   Votes attaching to shares
(a) Subject to any special rights or restrictions as to voting attached by or in accordance with the Articles to any shares or class of shares, on a show of hands every member who is present in person shall have one vote and on a poll every member who is present in person or by proxy shall have one vote for every share of which he is the holder.

   No voting rights where calls outstanding
(b) No member shall, unless the Board otherwise determines, be entitled to vote:

   (i)   if any call or other sum presently payable by him to the Company in respect of the shares remains unpaid; or

   (ii)   if a member has not paid to the Company all calls and other sums then payable by him in respect of shares in the Company, or by a member who has been served with a restriction notice after failure to provide the Company with information concerning interest in those shares required to be provided under the Act.

---

[43] POS Reg. Sch. 1, para. 32 requires "A summary of the provisions in the issuers memorandum of association determining its objects.
[44] POS Reg. Sch. 1, para. 11 requires "a description of the shares including the class and a description of the rights attaching to them including voting, dividends, return of capital on a winding up, redemption and a summary of the consents necessary for the variation of any of those rights."

A Practitioner's Guide to the Alternative Investment Market Rules

5.2   *Transfer of Shares*[45]

Transfer of securities without a written instrument
(a)   Title to and interest in securities may be transferred without a written instrument in accordance with statutory regulations from time to time made under the Act.[46]

Form of transfer
(b)   Transfers of shares may be effected by transfer in writing in any usual or common form or in any other form acceptable to the Board and may be under hand only. The instrument of transfer shall be signed by or on behalf of the transferor and (except in the case of fully paid shares) by or on behalf of the transferee. The transferor shall remain the holder of the shares concerned until the name of the transferee is entered in the register in respect of such shares.

Other rights to decline registration
(c)   The Board may decline to register any instrument of transfer unless:

   (i)   the duly stamped instrument of transfer:
      - is in respect of only one class of share;
      - is lodged at the registered office or such other place as the Board may appoint; and
      - is accompanied by the relevant share certificate(s) and such other evidence as the Board may reasonably require to show the right of the transferor to make the transfer; and

   (ii)   in the case of a transfer to joint holders, the number of joint holders does not exceed four.

(d)   The Board may also decline to register a transfer of shares (except for certain types of transfer) after there has been a failure to provide the Company with information concerning interest in those shares required to be provided under the Articles or the Act until such failure has been remedied.

---

[45] The securities must be free from restrictions on transferability subject to limited exceptions (AIM Rule 28. Also POS Reg. Sch. 1, para. 15 requires a description of "Any restrictions on the free transferability of the securities being offered."
[46] The POS Reg. Sch. 1, para. 15 requires a description of "Any restrictions on the free transferability of the securities being offered."

Appendix 1 – AIM Admission Document

5.3 Dividend
Final dividends
(a) the Company may by ordinary resolution declare dividends but no such dividends shall exceed the sum recommended by the Board.

Interim and fixed dividends
(b) In so far as, in the opinion of the Board, the profits of the Company justify such payments, the Board may declare and pay the fixed dividends on any class of shares carrying a fixed dividends expressed to be payable on fixed dates on the half-yearly or other dates prescribed for the payment of such dividends and may also from time to time declare and pay interim dividends on shares of any class of such sums and on such dates and in respect of such periods as it thinks fit.

Retention of dividends
(c) The Board may retain any dividend or other monies payable on or in respect of a share on which the Company has a lien, and may apply the same in or towards satisfaction of the debts, liabilities or engagements in respect of which the lien exists. The Board may withhold dividend payable on shares after there has been failure to provide the Company with information concerning interests in those shares required to be provided under the Act until such failure has been remedied.

Unclaimed dividend
(d) Any dividend unclaimed after a period of twelve years from the date the dividend became due for payment shall be forfeited and shall revert to the Company.

Distribution in specie
(e) the Company may upon the recommendation of the Board by ordinary resolution direct payment of a dividend in whole or in part by the distribution of specific assets (and in particular of paid-up shares or debentures of any other company) and the Board shall give effect to such resolution.

Distribution in specie on a winding up
(f) If the Company shall be wound up the liquidator may, with the authority of an extraordinary resolution and subject to any provision of law, divide among the members in specie or kind the whole or any part of the assets of the Company and whether or not the assets shall consist of property of one kind or shall consist of properties of different kinds, and may for

such purpose set such value as he deems fair upon any one of more class or classes or property and may determine how such division shall be carried out as between the members or different classes of members.

5.4 *Capitalisation of profits and reserves*

(a) The Board may, with the sanction of an ordinary resolution of the Company, capitalise any sum stranding to the credit of any of the Company's reserve accounts or any sum standing to the credit of profit and loss account.

(b) Such capitalisation shall be effected by appropriating such sum to the holders of ordinary shares in proportion to their holdings of ordinary shares and applying such sum on their behalf in paying up in full unissued shares.

5.5 *Overseas Members*

A member who (having no registered address within the United Kingdom) has not supplied to the Company an address within the United Kingdom for the service of notice shall not be entitled to receive notices from the Company.

5.6 *Share Capital*

Variation of rights
(a) The special rights attached to any class may, subject to the provisions of the Act, be varied either with the consent in writing of the holders of not less than three-quarters in nominal value of the issued shares of the class or with the sanction of an extraordinary resolution passed at a separate general meeting of the holders of the shares of the class.

Increase in share capital
(b) The Company may from time to time by ordinary resolution increase its share capital by such sum to be divided into shares of such amounts as the resolution shall prescribe.

Consolidation, subdivision and cancellation
(c) The Company may by ordinary resolution:

(i) consolidate and divide all or any of its share capital into shares of larger nominal value than its existing shares;

Appendix 1 – AIM Admission Document

      (ii)   subject to the provisions of the Act, sub-divide its shares.

Reduction or cancellation
(d) the Company may by special resolution reduce or cancel its share capital or any revaluation reserve or share premium account or any other reserve fund in any manner and with and subject to any confirmation or consent required by law.

Purchase of own shares
(e) Subject to the provisions of the Act, the Company may purchase or may enter into any contract under which it will or may purchase, any of its own shares.

5.7 *Forfeiture and Lien*

Notice on failure to pay a call
(a) If a member fails to pay in full any call or instalment of a call on the due date for payment the Board may at any time after the failure serve a notice on him requiring payment and shall state that in the event of non-payment in accordance with such notice the shares on which the call was made will be liable to be forfeited.

Lien on partly-paid shares
(b) the Company shall have a first and paramount lien on every share (not being a fully paid share) for all monies (whether presently payable or not) called or payable at a fixed time in respect of such share.

Sale of shares subject to lien
(c) the Company may sell in such manner as the Board thinks fit any share on which the Company has a lien, fourteen days after a notice in writing stating and demanding payment of the sum presently payable and giving notice of intention to sell.

5.8 *Directors*

Number of directors
(a) Unless otherwise determined by ordinary resolution the Directors shall not be fewer than two nor more than ten in number.

Directors' fees
(b) The ordinary remuneration of the non-executive Directors shall from time to time be determined by the Board.

Other remuneration of directors

(c) Any Director who holds any executive office or who serves on any committee of the Board, or who otherwise performs services which in the opinion of the Board are outside the scope of the ordinary duties of a Director, may be paid such extra remuneration by way of salary, commission or otherwise or may receive such other benefits as the Board may determine.

Directors' expenses

(d) The Board may repay to any director all such reasonable expenses as he may incur in attending meeting s of the Board or of any committee of the Board or shareholders' meetings or otherwise in connection with the business of the Company.

Directors' pensions and other benefits

(e) The Board has power to pay and agree to pay gratuities, pensions or other retirement, superannuation, death or disability benefits to (or to any person in respect of) any Director or ex-Director and for the purpose of providing any such gratuities, pensions or other benefits to contribute to any scheme or fund or to pay premiums.

Age limit

(f) Any provision of the Act which, subject to the provisions of the articles, would have the effect of rendering any person ineligible for appointment or election as a director or liable to vacate office as a director on account of his having reached any specified age or of requiring special notice or any other special formality in connection with the appointment or election of any Director over a specified age, shall not apply to the Company.

Restrictions on voting

(g) A Director shall not vote (save as provided in the articles) in respect of any contract or arrangement or any other proposal whatsoever in which he or persons connected with him have a material interest. A Director shall not be counted in the quorum at a meeting in relation to any resolution on which he is not entitled to vote.

(h) Subject to the provisions of the Act, a director shall be entitled to vote (and be counted in the quorum) in respect of any resolution:

    (i) relating to the giving of any security guarantee or indemnity in respect of:

Appendix 1 – AIM Admission Document

- money lent or obligations incurred by him or by any other person at the request of or for the benefit of the Company or any of its subsidiary undertakings; or
- a debt or obligation of the Company or any of its subsidiary undertakings for which he himself has assumed responsibility in whole or part under a guarantee or indemnity or by the giving of security;

(ii) where the Company or any of its subsidiary undertakings is offering securities on which offer the Director is or may be entitled to participate as a holder of securities or in the underwriting or sub-underwriting of which the Director is to participate;

(iii) relating to another company in which he does not hold an interest in shares representing one per cent or more of either any class of the equity share capital, or the voting rights in such company;

(iv) relating to a pension, superannuation or similar scheme or retirement, death or disability benefits scheme or employees' share scheme which has been approved by the Inland Revenue or is conditional upon such approval or does not aware him any privilege or benefit not awarded to the employee to whom such scheme relates; or

(v) concerning insurance which the Company proposes to maintain or purchase for the benefit of Directors or for the benefit of persons including Directors.

5.9 *Borrowing powers*

The Board may exercise all the powers of the Company to borrow money, to give guarantees and to mortgage or charge its undertaking, property and assets (present and future) and uncalled capital, and to issue debentures and other securities, whether outright or as collateral security for any debt, liability or obligation of the Company or of any third party.

5.10 *Untraceable members*

(a) the Company shall be entitled to cease sending dividend warrants by post if such warrants have been returned undelivered or left uncashed, provided that his power may not be exercised until either such warrants have been so returned or left uncashed on two consecutive occasions or, following one such occasion, reasonable enquiries have failed to establish any new address of the registered holder.

(b) the Company shall be entitled to sell subject to various notice requirements at the best price reasonably obtainable at the time of sale the shares of a member if during a period of 12 years no communication has been received by the Company from the member and no cheque or warrant sent by the Company in respect of the shares has been cashed and no fewer than three dividends in respect of the shares have become payable and no dividend in respect of those shares have been claimed.

6. Directors' and other interests

6.1 *Directors' and other significant interests in the Company's share capital*[47]

(a) At the date of this document and immediately following the Offer for Subscription, the interests of the Directors (including persons connected with them within the meaning of section 346 of the Act) in the issued share capital of the Company, which have been notified to the Company pursuant to sections 324 and 328 of the Act and which are shown in the register of Directors' interests maintained under section 325 of the Act, are as follows:

Directors	At the date of this document	Immediately following the Offer for Subscription
•	• (•%)	• (•%)
•	• (•%)	• (•%)
•	• (•%)	• (•%)
•	• (•%)	• (•%)

---

[47] POS Reg. Sch. 1, para. 47(2) requires "The interests of each director of the issuer in the share capital of the issuer, distinguishing between beneficial and non-beneficial interests or an appropriate negative statement".

Appendix 1 – AIM Admission Document

In addition Options have been granted to Directors as follows :

Name	No or Ordinary Shares under Option	Date of Grant	Expiry date of Option	Exercise price per Ordinary Share

(b) All the above interests of the Directors are or will be beneficial.

(c) At the date of this document and immediately following the Offer for Subscription, insofar as known to the Directors, the only persons who are interested directly or indirectly in 3% or more of the capital of the Company, together with the amount, expressed as a percentage, of each such person's interest other than the New Ordinary Shares are as follows:

Shareholders	At the date of this document	Immediately following the Offer for Subscription
•*	• (•%)	• (•%)
•*	• (•%)	• (•%)
•*	• (•%)	• (•%)
•	• (•%)	• (•%)

* denotes directors

(d) Save as described above, the Directors are not aware of any person who, directly or indirectly, jointly or severally, exercise or could exercise control over the Company.[48]

6.2 *Directors' remuneration and service agreements*[49]

(a) The aggregate remuneration and benefits in kind of the directors of [Subsidiary] in respect of the financial year ended • was £•. The

---

[48] POS Reg para 40 requires "Insofar as the offeror has the information, an indication of the person, who, directly or indirectly, jointly or severally, exercise or could exercise control over the issuer and particulars of the proportion of the issuer's voting capital held by such person." Also AIM Rule Sch. 2(h) requires the name of the person who, insofar as known to its directors, is interested directly or indirectly in 3 per cent or more of its capital, together with the amount, expressed as a percentage, of each such person's interest.

[49] POS Reg. Sch. 1, para. 46 requires "A concise description of the directors' existing or proposed service contracts with the issuer or any subsidiary of the issuer, excluding contracts expiring, or determinable by the employing company without payment of compensation within one year, or an appropriate negative statement. Also POS Reg 47(1) requires "The aggregate remuneration paid and benefits in kind granted to the directors of the issuer during the last completed financial year of the issuer, together with an estimate of the aggregate amount payable and benefits in kind to be granted to the directors, and proposed directors, for the current financial year under the arrangements in force at the date on which the offer is first made."

A Practitioner's Guide to the Alternative Investment Market Rules

aggregate remuneration and benefits in kind of the directors of the Group in respect of the financial year ending • under the arrangements in force at the date hereof is expected to be £•.

(b) Service contracts (or in the case of the chairman and non-executive director, letters of appointment) have been entered into between the Company and the Directors, the principal terms of which are summarised below:

Directors	Effective Date of Contract	Current Annual Remuneration	Pension Contribution % of Salary	Position
•		£•	•%	Managing Director
•		£•	•%	Marketing Director
•		£•	•%	Finance Director
•		£•	•%	Chairman
•		£•	•%	Non-Executive Director

(c) All service agreements are terminable on 12 months' notice by either party. Following admission, there will be no other existing or proposed service contracts between any of the Directors and any member of the Group.

(d) There are no service agreements existing or proposed between the Directors and the Company or any of its subsidiaries which are not terminable within one year by the relevant company without payment of compensation (other than statutory compensation).

(e) There is no arrangement under which any Director has agreed to waive future emoluments nor has there been any waiver of emoluments during the financial year immediately preceding the date of this document.

6.3 *Loans and guarantees*

There are no loans or guarantees provided by any member of the Group for the benefit of any director.

Appendix 1 – AIM Admission Document

6.4　*Directors' interests in transactions*

Save as disclosed in this document, no Director has or has had any interest in any transaction which is of an unusual nature, contains unusual terms or is significant in relation to the business of the Group and which was effected during the current or immediately preceding financial year or during any earlier financial year and remains in any respect outstanding or unperformed.

6.5　*Directorships*[50]

(a)　In addition to the Company and [Subsidiary], the Directors hold, and have previously held the following directorships:

[Director]

Current directorships

-

Former directorships in previous five years

-

• [Director]

Current directorships

-

---

[50] AIM Rule Sch. 2(f) requires the following information relating to each director and each proposed director:
   (i)　the director's full name, any previous names and age;
   (ii)　the names of all companies and partnerships of which the director has been a director or partner at any time in the previous five years, indicating whether or not the director is still a director or partner;
   (iii)　any unspent convictions in relation to indictable offences;
   (iv)　details of any bankruptcies or individual voluntary arrangements of such director;
   (v)　details of any receiverships, compulsory liquidations, creditors voluntary liquidations, administrations, company voluntary arrangements or any composition or arrangement with its creditors generally or any class of its creditors of any company where such director was a director at the time of or within the 12 months preceding such events;
   (vi)　details of any compulsory liquidations, administrations or partnership voluntary arrangements of any partnerships where such director was a partner at the time of or within the 12 months preceding such events;
   (vii)　details of receiverships of any asset of such director or of a partnership of which the director was a partner at the time of or within the 12 months preceding such events; and
   (viii)　details of any public criticisms of such director by statutory or regulatory authorities (including recognised professional bodies), and whether such director has ever been disqualified by a court from acting as a director of a company or from acting in the management or conduct of the affairs of any company.

Former directorships in previous five years

•

• [Director]

Current directorships

None apart from [Subsidiary] and [Company Name]

Former directorships in previous five years

•

[Director]

Current directorships

None apart from [Subsidiary] and [Company Name]
Former directorships in previous five years

(b) Save as disclosed above none of the Directors has been a director or partner at any time in the previous five years. None of the Directors has any unspent convictions in respect of indictable offences. None of the Directors has been a bankrupt or entered into an individual voluntary arrangement. None of the Directors was a partner of any partnership at the time of or within 12 months of any compulsory liquidation, administration or partnership voluntary arrangement. None of the Directors has owned an asset over which a receiver has been appointed nor has any of the Directors been a partner of any partnership at the time of or within 12 months of receivership of any assets of the partnership.

(c) There have been no public criticisms of any of the Directors by any statutory or regulatory authority (including recognised professional bodies) and none of the directors has ever been disqualified by a court from acting as a director of a company or from acting in the management or conduct of the affairs of any company.

Appendix 1 – AIM Admission Document

(d) None of the Directors was a director of any company at the time of or within 12 months preceding any receivership, compulsory liquidation, creditors voluntary liquidation, administration, company voluntary arrangement or any composition or arrangements with its creditors generally or any class of its creditors [save as disclosed below:]

-
-

7. **Share Option Scheme**

7.1 *The main features of the scheme*

The Board adopted the rules constituting the share option scheme by a resolution passed on •. The scheme is intended to motivate, retain and reward selected directors, employees and consultants who by their efforts are able to influence the performance and success of the Company's business. This scheme has not been approved by the Inland Revenue.

7.2 *Eligibility*

All employees, directors and consultants are eligible to participate. No eligible person is entitled to participate as of right. The selection of those eligible who are to participate is within the discretion of the board of directors.

7.3 *Limit on number of shares*

The Company may not grant an option under the share option scheme if, as a result, the number of shares issued or issuable in respect of all options granted under this share option scheme and any other share option scheme or employees' share scheme operated by the Company would, as a result of options or rights granted within the preceding ten year period, exceed 10% of the ordinary share capital of the Company.

7.4 *Acquisition price*

The price per ordinary share at which an option may be exercised under the scheme shall not be less than the greater of its nominal value, the Offer Price or its market value on the day the invitation to apply for an option was issued.

7.5 Time at which invitations may be issued

The Company may invite eligible employees to apply for an option within six weeks after either the date the scheme is adopted by the Company in general meeting or the date on which the annual or half-yearly results of the Company are announced, and in any event no later than the tenth anniversary of the date that the scheme is adopted by the Company.

7.6 Exercise of options

An option under the share option scheme cannot be exercised more than ten years after the date on which it was granted, nor can it normally be exercised less than three years after its grant. However, options may be exercised (whether the initial three year period has expired or not) in the following circumstances:

(a) the participant is deceased, in which case his personal representatives may exercise the option within one year after the date of death, failing which the option will lapse;

(b) the participant ceases to be employed by reason of injury, disability, redundancy, or retirement in which case a participant may exercise his option no later than three months from the date of such termination of employment failing which the option will lapse;

(c) if the Company passes a resolution for voluntary winding up, any subsisting option may be exercised within six months after the date upon which the resolution is passed;

(d) if the participant is adjudicated bankrupt, in which event the option will lapse immediately; or

(e) if as a result of a general offer a third party obtains control of the Company, the option is exercisable for a period of six months after such control has been obtained, although with the consent of the acquiring company, the existing option may be replaced by a new option over shares in the acquiring company or some other qualifying company.

Appendix 1 – AIM Admission Document

7.7 **General**

(a) If the Company undertakes a capitalisation or rights issue or any consolidation, sub-division or reduction of its ordinary share capital, the number of shares subject to any option and the acquisition price of those shares shall be adjusted in such manner as the auditors of the Company confirm to be fair and reasonable.

(b) Participation in the share option scheme does not afford to any participant any additional right to compensation on the termination of his employment.

(c) Save in general for minor amendments designed to benefit the administration of the share option scheme, to take account of a change in legislation or to obtain or maintain favourable tax, exchange control or regulatory treatment for participants in the scheme or for the Company, no alteration to the advantage of participants in the scheme may be made without the prior approval of shareholders in general meeting.

8. **Premises**

Details of the principal properties occupied by the Group are as follows:

Location	Tenure	Rent	Lease Expiry Date
•	•	•	•

9. **Material Contracts**[51]

The following contracts, not being contracts entered into in the ordinary course of business, have been entered into by a member of the Group [in the two years prior to the date hereof] and are, or may be, material:

(a) Share for share exchange agreement referred to at paragraph • above, relating to the acquisition by the company of the entire issued share capital of [Subsidiary].

(b) The option agreement referred to in paragraph • above.

---

[51] Subject to limited exceptions, where an applicant's main activity is a business which has not been independent and earning revenue for at least two years, it must ensure that all related parties and applicable employees as at the date of admission agree not to dispose of any interest in its securities for one year from the admission of its securities. (AIM Rule 7).

(c) The lease referred to at paragraph • above.

(d) Agreement dated • between the Company (1) [Nominated Adviser] (2) [Broker] (3) and the Directors (4) (the "placing agreement") under which [Broker] has agreed to use its reasonable endeavours to procure places on behalf of the Company to subscribe for Ordinary Shares at the Offer Price. The Directors have given certain representations, warranties and indemnities as to the accuracy of the information contained in this document and other matters in relation to the Company and its business. The placing agreement is conditional upon the minimum amount being raised and upon the entire issued share capital of the company being admitted to trading on AIM.

(e) Agreement dated • between the Company (1) [Broker] (2) and the persons referred to in the schedule to the agreement (3) (the "Restricted Persons Agreement") the Directors, associates of the Directors, employees of the Company and associates of such employees [(except those who hold any interest in less than 1% of the ordinary shares of the company)] agreed not to dispose of any interest in their ordinary shares for a period of one year from the date of admission to trading on AIM, save in the event of an intervening court order, a takeover offer relating to the Company's shares becoming or being declared unconditional or on the death of the director or employee.

10. **Litigation**[52]

There are no legal or arbitration proceedings (including any such proceedings which are pending or threatened of which the Group is aware) against, or being brought by, the Company or any member of the Group which are having or may have a significant effect on the Company's financial position.

11. **Working Capital**[53]

The Directors are of the opinion that, having made due and careful enquiry, the working capital available to the Company and the Group will, be sufficient for the Company's present requirements, that it for at least twelve months from the date of Admission.

---

[52] POS Reg. Sch. 1, para. 44 requires "Information on any legal or arbitration proceedings, active, pending or threatened against, or being brought by, the issuer or any member of its group which are having or may have a significant affect on the issuers' financial position."

[53] This is not a requirement of the POS Regs but is a requirement of the AIM Rules (AIM Rule Sch. 2 (b)).

Appendix 1 – AIM Admission Document

12.   **United Kingdom Taxation**[54]

The following statements are intended only as a general guide to current United Kingdom tax legislation and to what is understood to be the current practice of the United Kingdom Inland Revenue (the "Inland Revenue") and may not apply to certain classes of shareholder (such as dealers in securities). Any person who is in any doubt as to his tax position is strongly recommended to consult his professional advisers immediately.

Taxation of Dividends

There is no United Kingdom withholding tax on dividends. An individual Shareholder resident in the UK for tax purposes will be taxable on the total of any dividend received and the related tax credit (the "gross dividend"), which will be regarded as the top slice of the individual's income.

The tax credit on dividends paid by the company is reduced to one-ninth of the dividend paid (or ten per cent of the gross dividend). However, individuals who are not liable to tax at the higher rate will have no further liability and for higher rate taxpayers, the higher rate is 32.5 per cent rather than 40 per cent. This means that a higher rate Shareholder receiving a dividend of £90 will be treated as having gross income of £100 (the net dividend of £90 plus a tax credit of £10) and after allowing for the tax credit of £10 will have a further £22.50 liability. The same procedure applies for UK resident trustees save that the rate applicable to trusts will be 25 per cent (as opposed to 32.5 per cent).

Generally, Shareholders are not entitled to reclaim the tax credit attaching to any dividends paid by the company. Certain transitional relief applies to dividends received by charities up to the tax year ended 5 April 2004.

Subject to certain exceptions for traders in securities, a Shareholder that is a company resident for tax purposes in the United Kingdom will not be chargeable to tax on dividends received from the Company.

UK pension funds are not entitled to reclaim any part of the tax credit associated with dividends paid by the Company.

---

[54] POS Reg.Sch.1.para.13 requires "Particulars of tax on income from the securities withheld at source, including tax credits". The taxation section must be reviewed by the tax adviser to the issuer.

Entitlement to claim repayment of any part of a tax credit for Shareholders not resident in the UK for tax purposes will depend, in general, on the existence and terms of any double tax convention between the United Kingdom and the country in which the holder is resident. Such Shareholders should not, however, that since 6 April 1999, most Shareholders who had previously been able to claim repayment of any part of the tax credit have either ceased to be able to claim such repayment or the amounts repayable are less than one per cent of the dividend. Shareholders who are not resident in the United Kingdom should consult their own tax advisers concerning their tax liability on dividends received, whether they are entitled to claim repayment of any part of the tax credit and, if so, the procedure for so doing.

Stamp Duty / Stamp Duty Reserve Tax

Under the issue arrangements, no stamp duty or stamp duty reserve tax ("SDRT") will be payable by applicants on the issue of Ordinary Shares under the Offer for Subscription.

The conveyance or transfer on sale of Ordinary Shares will generally be liable to stamp duty on the instrument of transfer, at a rate of 50p per £100 (or part thereof) on the amount or value of the consideration. Where an unconditional agreement to transfer such shares is not completed by a duly stamped instrument of transfer a charge to SDRT (generally at the same rate) will arise. Stamp duty and SDRT are usually paid by the purchaser.

The statements made in the paragraphs above are intended as a general guide only to current UK taxation law and Inland Revenue practice and may not apply to certain classes of persons (such as dealers in securities).

Any person who is in any doubt as to his tax position, and in particular any person who is subject to taxation in a jurisdiction other than the United Kingdom is strongly advised to consult his professional adviser.

Appendix 1 – AIM Admission Document

13. **General**[55]

13.1 Save as disclosed in this document no person (other than professional advisers named in this document and trade suppliers) has:

(a) received, directly or indirectly, from the Company within the 12 months preceding the application for Admission to; or

(b) entered into contractual arrangements (not otherwise disclosed in this document) to receive, directly or indirectly, from the Company on or after Admission

any of the following:

(i) fees totalling £10,000 or more;
(ii) securities in the Company where these have a value of £10,000 or more calculated by reference to the Offer Price; or
(iii) any other benefit with the value of £10,000 or more at the date of Admission.

13.2 [[Nominated Adviser] has been appointed nominated adviser to the Company. Under the AIM rules the nominated adviser owes certain responsibilities to the London Stock Exchange. In accordance with these rules, [Nominated Adviser] has confirmed to the London Stock Exchange that it has satisfied itself that the Directors of the Company have received independent advice and guidance as to the nature of their responsibilities and obligations under the rules and that, to the best of its knowledge and belief, all relevant requirements of the AIM rules (save for compliance with Regulation 9 of the Regulations in respect of which the nominated adviser is not required to satisfy itself) have been complied with. [Nominated Adviser] has also satisfied itself that the contents of this document have been appropriately verified. In giving its confirmation to the London Stock Exchange, [Nominated Adviser] has not made its own enquiries except as to matters which have come to its attention and on which it considered it necessary to satisfy itself. No liability whatsoever

---

[55] The AIM prospectus must contain the name of any person (excluding professional advisers otherwise disclosed in the admission document and trade suppliers) who has:
(i) received, directly or indirectly, from it within the 12 months preceding the application for admission to trading on AIM; or
(ii) entered into contractual arrangements (not otherwise disclosed in the admission document) to receive, directly or indirectly, from it on or after admission any of the following:
- fees totalling £10,000 or more;
- its securities where these have a value of £10,000 or more calculated by reference to the issue price or, in the case of an introduction, the opening price; or
- any other benefit with a value of £10,000 or more at the date of admission,

giving full details of the relationship of such person with the applicant and of the fees, securities or other benefit received or to be received (AIM Rule Sch. 2(g)).

A Practitioner's Guide to the Alternative Investment Market Rules

is accepted by [Nominated Adviser] for the accuracy of any information or opinions contained in this document or for the omission of any material information, for which the Company and its Directors are solely responsible.] [[Nominated Adviser] does not regard themselves as being a "responsible person" (as that term is used in the POS Regulations) in relation to this document.]

13.3 [Nominated Adviser] has given and has not withdrawn its written consent to the issue of this document with the inclusion of its name in the form and context in which it appears.

13.4 [Nominated Adviser], which is a member of [The Securities and Futures Authority Limited], has its registered office at •.

13.5 [Broker] has been appointed as broker to the Company. [Broker] is registered in England and Wales with number • and its registered office is at • and they are authorised by the Securities & Futures Authority Ltd in the conduct of investment business.

13.6 The estimated amount of the expenses of the Offer which are all payable by the Company, assuming the Offer is fully subscribed, is £• (excluding VAT). This amount includes an estimated commission of £• payable by the Company to any person in consideration of his agreeing to subscribe for securities to which the prospectus relates or of his procuring or agreeing to procure subscriptions for such securities.[56]

13.7 The minimum amount[57] of £• , must in the opinion of the Directors, be raised by the Offer for Subscription in order to provide the sums required to be provided in respect of each of the following:

(a) the purchase price of any property purchased, or to be purchased, which is to be defrayed in whole or in part out of the proceeds of the issue: £nil

(b) any preliminary expenses payable by the Company and any commission so payable to any person in consideration of his agreeing to subscribe for or of his procuring or agreeing to procure subscription for, any shares in the Company: £•

(c) the repayment of any money borrowed by the Company in respect of any of the foregoing matters: £•

---

[56] See POS Reg. Sch.1, para. 23.
[57] See POS Reg. Sch.1, para. 21(a).

Appendix 1 – AIM Admission Document

(d) working capital: £•

No amounts are to be provided in respect[58] of the matters mentioned in this paragraph otherwise than out of the proceeds of the Offer for Subscription.

13.8 [Name of auditor],[59] [the address of auditor] the auditors of the Company and [Subsidiary], have given and have not withdrawn their written consent to the inclusion of their reports in this document and accept responsibility[60] for them and have stated that they have not become aware, since the date of any report, of any matter affecting the validity of that report at that date.[61]

13.9 [The financial information contained in this document[62] does not constitute full statutory accounts as referred to in section 240 of the Act. Statutory audited accounts of [Subsidiary] for the last two financial years to which the financial information relates and on which the auditors gave reports under section 235 of the Act, which were neither qualified within the meaning of section 262 of the Act nor contained statements under section 237(2) or (3) of the Act, have been delivered to the Registrar of Companies. The statutory financial statements for the period ended • were given an unqualified [exemption] report.]

13.10 Save as disclosed in this document there has been no significant change in the financial or trading position of the Group since •, the date to which the latest audited financial statements were made up.

13.11 The Offer is [not] underwritten or guaranteed.[63]

13.12 Save as disclosed in this document, no payment (including commissions) or other benefit has been or is to be paid or given to any promoter of the Company.

13.13 The net proceeds assuming full subscription are estimated at £• for the Company.

13.14 The current accounting reference period of the Company will end on •.

---

[58] See POS Reg. Sch.1 para. 21(b).
[59] Required by POS Reg. Sch.1, para.45(1)(a)(ii).
[60] The names, addresses and functions of those persons responsible for the prospectus or any part of the prospectus is required by POS Reg. Sch. 1, para. 9 (and see also para. 10(2)).
[61] Required by POS Reg. Para. 45(1)(a)(iv).
[62] The published accounts must be prepared in accordance with United Kingdom or United States generally accepted accounting practice or International Accounting Standards. (AIM Rule 17).
[63] POS Reg. Sch. 1, para. 22 requires "The names of any persons underwriting or guaranteeing the offer".

A Practitioner's Guide to the Alternative Investment Market Rules

14. **Publication**

    Copies of this document will be available free of charge to the public at the offices of [Company's Solicitors] from the date of this document until at least the end of the period during which the Offer for Subscription remains open or if later for one month.[64]

15. **Documents Available for Inspection**

    Copies of the following documents may be inspected at the offices of [solicitors] during the usual business hours on any weekday (weekends and public holidays excepted) for the period of 14 days following the date of this document:

    (a) the Memorandum and Articles of Association of the Company;

    (b) the audited accounts of [Subsidiary] for the periods ended • and •;

    (c) the option agreement referred to at paragraph • above;

    (d) the Directors' service agreements and letter of appointment referred to in paragraph • above;

    (e) the Share Option Scheme;

    (f) the […….. Agreement] referred to in paragraph • above;

    (g) the material contracts referred to in paragraph • above;

    (h) the written consents referred to in paragraph • above;

    Date:[65]

---

[64] See POS Reg. 4(1). Also see AIM Rule 18.
[65] POS Reg. Sch. 1, para. 5 requires "The date of publication of the prospectus."

Appendix 1 – AIM Admission Document

PART SIX
TERMS AND CONDITIONS OF APPLICATION[66]

1. **Completion of Application Form**

    If you with to apply for New Ordinary Shares you must complete an Application Form in accordance with the instructions accompanying that form.

2. **Number of applications**

    Only one application can be made by you (or on your behalf) and for your benefit on an Application Form. Multiple applications or suspected multiple applications are liable to be rejected.

3. **Allocation of New Ordinary Shares**

    The basis of allocation will be determined by [the Company] [Nominated Adviser in consultation with the Directors] in its absolute discretion. The right is reserved to reject in whole or in part and/or scale down any application or any part thereof. The right is also reserved to treat as valid any application not in all respects completed in accordance with the instructions relating to the Application Form including if the accompanying cheque or banker's draft is for the wrong amount. Dealings prior to the issue of share certificates will be at the risk of applicants. A person so dealing must recognise the risk that an application may not have been accepted to the extent anticipated or at all.

4. **Expected despatch of definitive share certificates**

    The expected date for despatch of definitive share certificates[67] in respect of New Ordinary Shares will be •. [It is anticipated that trading in the Ordinary Shares on AIM should commence on •.

5. **Joint application**

    In the case of a joint application, references to you in these terms and conditions of application are to each of you, and your liability is joint and several.

---

[66] This section only required if an offer (and is not required if all shares are being placed).
[67] POS Reg. Sch. 1, para. 27 requires "The arrangements for payment for the securities being offered and the arrangements for the timetable for their delivery".

6. Conditions to be satisfied

The contract created by the acceptance of the applications under the Offer (other than as mentioned in paragraph 9(b) [honouring of cheques] below) will be conditional upon:-

(a) the Receiving Agents receiving the Minimum Amount by 3.00 pm on •, or such later date as the Board may resolve, which in any event shall be no later than •;

(b) Admission becoming effective by no later than 9.30 am on •; and

(c) the Placing Agreement referred to in paragraph • of Part IV of this document becoming wholly unconditional and not being terminated before Admission.

7. Application moneys

The right is reserved by the Company to present all cheques and banker's drafts for payment on receipt and to retain share certificates and surplus application moneys pending clearance of successful applicants' cheques and banker's drafts. If any application is not accepted (either in whole or in part) or if any contract created by acceptance does not become fully unconditional, the application moneys or, as the case may be, the balance thereof will be returned (without interest) within 10 days of the closing date of the Offer[68] by returning each relevant applicant's cheque or banker's draft or by crossed cheque in favour of the first-named applicant, through the post at the risk of the person(s) entitled thereto. In the meantime, application moneys will be retained by the Receiving Agents in a separate account.

8. Money Laundering Regulations

It is a term of the Offer for Subscription that, to ensure compliance with the Money Laundering Regulations 1993 the Company and/or the Receiving Agent is entitled to require, at its absolute discretion, verification of identity from any applicant for Ordinary Shares including, without limitation, any applicant who either (i) tenders payment by way of a cheque or banker's draft drawn on an account in the name of a person or persons other than the applicant or (ii) appears to the Company or the

---

[68] POS Reg. Sch. 1, para. 28 requires "The arrangements during the period prior to the delivery of the securities being offered relating to the moneys received from applicants including the arrangements for the return of moneys to applicants where their applications are not accepted in whole or in part and the timetable for the return of such moneys". See also POS Reg. Sch.1, para.27.

Appendix 1 – AIM Admission Document

Receiving Agent to be acting on behalf of some other person. Pending the provision of evidence satisfactory to the Receiving Agent as to the identity of the applicant and/or any person on whose behalf the applicant appears to be acting, the Receiving Agent may, in its absolute discretion, retain an Application Form lodged by an applicant and/or the cheque or other remittance relating thereto and/or not enter the applicant on the register of members or issue any certificate in respect of Ordinary Shares allotted to the applicant.

If verification of identity is required, this may result in a delay in dealing with an application and in rejection of the application. The Company reserves the right, in its absolute discretion, for it or the Receiving Agent to reject any application in respect of which the Receiving Agent considers that, having requested verification of identity, it has not received evidence of such identity satisfactory to it by such time as may be specified in the request for verification of identity or in any event within a reasonable period. In the event of an application being rejected in any such circumstances, the Company reserves the right in its absolute discretion, but shall have no obligation, to terminate any contract of allotment relating to or constituted by the Application Form (in which event the money payable or paid in respect of the application will be returned (without interest) to the account of the bank from which such sums were original debited) and/or to endeavour to procure other subscribers for the Ordinary Shares in question (but in each case without prejudice to any rights the Company may have to take proceedings to recover in respect of loss or damage suffered or incurred by it as a result of the failure to produce satisfactory evidence as aforesaid). The submission of an Application Form will constitute a warranty and undertaking by the applicant to provide promptly to the Company or the Receiving Agent such information as may be specified by it as being required for the purpose of the Money Laundering Regulations 1993.

Neither the Company nor the Receiving Agent shall be responsible or have any liability for loss or damage (whether actual or alleged) arising from the election by the Company or the Receiving Agent to treat an application in respect of Ordinary Shares lodged by any applicant as invalid or to terminate the contract of allotment as a result of the Company or the Receiving Agent not having received evidence as to the identity of the applicant reasonably satisfactory to it within a reasonable time of having requested such information.

9. **General terms**

By completing and delivering an Application Form, you, as the applicant (and, if you sign the Application Form on behalf of somebody else or a corporation, that person or corporation, except as referred to in paragraphs (f) and (h) below):

(a) offer to subscribe for the number of New Ordinary Shares specified in your Application Form (or such lesser number for which your application is accepted) at the Offer Price on the terms of and subject to the Prospectus;

(b) warrant that your cheque or banker's draft will be honoured on first presentation and agree that if it is not so honoured you will not be entitled to receive a share certificate in respect of the shares applied for or to enjoy or receive any rights or distributions in respect of such shares unless and until you make payment in cleared funds for such shares and such payment is accepted by the Company in its absolute discretion (which acceptance shall be on the basis that you indemnify it against all costs, damages, losses, expenses and liabilities arising out of or in connection with the failure of your remittance to be honoured on first presentation) and you agree that, at any time prior to the unconditional acceptance by the Company of such later payment, the Company may (without prejudice to its other rights) avoid the agreement to subscribe such shares and may allot such shares to some other person, in which case you will not be entitled to any payment in respect of such shares other than the refund to you at your risk of any proceeds of the cheque or banker's draft accompanying your application, without interest;

(c) agree that, in respect of those New Ordinary Shares for which your application has been received and is not rejected, acceptance of your application shall be constituted by notification of acceptance thereof to the Receiving Agents;

(d) agree that any moneys returnable to you may be retained by the Receiving Agent pending clearance of your remittance and that such moneys will not bear interest;

(e) authorise the Receiving Agent to send share certificate(s) in respect of the number of New Ordinary Shares for which your application is accepted and/or a crossed cheque for any moneys returnable, by post, without interest, at the risk of the person(s) entitled thereto, to the address of the person (or in the case of joint holders the first-named person)

Appendix 1 – AIM Admission Document

named as an applicant in the Application Form and to procure that your name (together with the name(s) of any other joint applicant(s)) is/are placed on the register of members of the Company in respect of such New Ordinary Shares;

(f) warrant that, if you sign the Application Form on behalf of somebody else or on behalf of a corporation, you have due authority to do so on behalf of that other person or corporation, and such person or corporation will also be bound accordingly and will be deemed also to have given the confirmations, warranties and undertakings contained herein and undertake to enclose your power of attorney or a copy thereof duly certified by a solicitor with the Application Form;

(g) agree that all applications, acceptances of applications and contracts resulting therefrom under the Offer shall be governed by and construed in accordance with English law, and that you submit to the jurisdiction of the English Courts and agree that nothing shall limit the right of the Company to bring any action, suit or proceeding arising out of or in connection with any such applications, acceptances of applications and contracts in any other manner permitted by law or in any court of competent jurisdiction;

(h) confirm that, in making such application, neither you nor any person on whose behalf you are applying are relying on any information or representation in relation to the Company other than the information contained in the Prospectus;

(i) authorise the Receiving Agents or any person authorised by them, as your agent, to do all things necessary to effect registration of any New Ordinary Shares subscribed by you into your name(s) or into the name(s) of any person(s) in whose favour the entitlement to any such Ordinary Shares has been transferred and authorise any representative of the Receiving Agents to execute any document required therefor;

(j) agree that, having had the opportunity to read the Prospectus, you shall be deemed to have had notice of all information and representations concerning the Company and the Ordinary Shares contained therein;

(k) confirm and warrant that you have read and complied with paragraph 10 below;

(l) confirm that you have reviewed the restrictions contained in paragraph 11 below and warrant as provided therein;

(m) confirm that you are not under the age of 18;

(n) agree that all documents and cheques sent by post to, by or on behalf of the Company or the Receiving Agents, will be sent at the risk of the person(s) entitled thereto;

(o) agree, on request by the Company or at its discretion on behalf of the Company, to disclose promptly in writing to it, any information which it may reasonably request in connection with your application and authorise it to disclose any information relating to your application as it considers appropriate; and

(p) warrant that no other application has been made by you for your own account or by another person on your behalf or for your benefit and with your knowledge for such purpose or, if you are applying as agent or nominee of another person, that no other application is being made by you (not being an application as aforesaid) as an agent or nominee for another person and that such other person is not, to your knowledge, acting in concert with any other person or persons as aforesaid.

10. **Non-UK applicants**

No person receiving a copy of this Prospectus or an Application Form in any territory other than the UK may treat the same as constituting an invitation or offer to him, nor should he in any event use such Application Form unless, in the relevant territory, such an invitation or offer could lawfully be made to him or such Application Form could lawfully be used without contravention of any registration or other legal requirements. It is the responsibility of any person outside the UK wishing to make an application hereunder to satisfy himself as to full observance of the laws of any relevant territory in connection therewith, including obtaining any requisite governmental or other consents, observing any other formalities requiring to be observed in such territory and paying any issue, transfer or other taxes requires to be paid in such territory.

11. **United States**

The New Ordinary Shares have not been and will not be registered under the United States Securities Act of 1933 (as amended) and, subject to certain exceptions, the New Ordinary Shares may not be offered, sold, transferred or delivered, directly or indirectly, in the United States or to any US Person. Persons subscribing for New Ordinary Shares (unless they satisfy the Company that New Ordinary Shares can be allotted

Appendix 1 – AIM Admission Document

without breach of United States securities laws) represent and warrant to the Company that they are not a person in the United States and they are not subscribing for New Ordinary Shares for the account of any such person and will not offer, sell, renounce, transfer or deliver, directly or indirectly, such New Ordinary Shares in the United States or to any such person. As used herein, "United States" means the United States of America (including the States thereof and the District of Columbia), its territories and possessions and "US Person" means any person or entity defined as such in Rule 902(o) under the Securities Act of 1933 and, without limiting the generality of the foregoing, US Person includes a natural person resident in the United States (including any State thereof) and an estate or trust, if any executor, administrator or trustee is a US Person, but shall not include a branch or agency of a US Person located outside the United States if such agency or branch operates for valid business reasons and is engaged in the business of insurance or banking and is subject to substantive insurance or banking regulation, respectively, in the jurisdiction where located. The Company has not been and will not be registered under the United States Investment Company Act of 1940 (as amended).

12. **Definitions**

    Save where the context otherwise requires, words and expressions defined in the Prospectus have the same meanings when used in the Application Form and any explanatory notes in relation thereto.

A Practitioner's Guide to the Alternative Investment Market Rules

HOW TO COMPLETE THE APPLICATION FORM

Before making any application to acquire Ordinary Shares, you are recommended to consult an independent financial adviser authorised under the Financial Services Act 1986. The following instructions should be read in conjunction with the Application Form and the terms and conditions of application set out in this document.

13. **Insert in Box 1 (in figures) the number of Ordinary Shares for which you are applying.**

14. **Insert in Box 2 (in figures) the amount of your cheque or banker's draft.**

15. **Insert your full name and address in BLOCK CAPITALS in Box 3.**

16. **Sign and date the Application Form in Box 4.**

    The Application Form may be signed by another person on your behalf (and/or on behalf of any joint applicant(s)) if that person is duly authorised to do so, but the power(s) of attorney (or (a) copy(ies) thereof duly certified by a solicitor) or form(s) of authority must be enclosed for inspection. A corporation should sign under the hand of a duly authorised official whose representative capacity must be stated.

17. **You must pin a single cheque or banker's draft to your completed Application Form in Box 5. Your cheque or banker's draft must be payable to "•" for the amount payable on application (inserted in Box 2) and should be crossed "A/C payee only".**

    A separate cheque or banker's draft must accompany each application. No other method of payment is acceptable. No receipt will be issued for this payment.

    Your cheque or banker's draft must be drawn in Sterling and bear a UK bank sorting code in the top right-hand corner.

18. **You may apply jointly with up to three other persons.**

    If you are applying jointly you must arrange for the Application Form to be completed by or on behalf of each joint applicant. Their full names and addresses should be inserted in BLOCK CAPITALS in Box 6.

Appendix 1 – AIM Admission Document

19. Box 7 must be signed by or on behalf of each joint applicant (other than the first applicant who should complete Box 3 and sign Box 4).

    Send the completed Application Form by post or by hand to • (ref: •) duly completed.

A Practitioner's Guide to the Alternative Investment Market Rules

APPLICATION FORM
[Company Name]

IMPORTANT: Before completing this Application Form you should read the above terms and conditions of application and the above notes on how to complete the Application Form. Boxes 1-4 must be completed by all applicants. Your remittance must be pinned at Box 5. Boxes 6 and 7 must also be completed in the case of joint applicants. Applications must be for a minimum of • Ordinary Shares [and a maximum of • Ordinary Shares]. Applications must be made in multiples of • Ordinary Shares.

PLEASE RETURN YOUR COMPLETED APPLICATION FORM BY POST TO, OR DELIVER IT TO, • (ref: •).

IN EACH CASE IT MUST ARRIVE NOT LATER THAN •pm on •, unless extended by the Directors.

I/We offer to subscribe for		Ordinary Shares at £1 each	1

in [**Company Name**] on the terms and subject to the conditions of application set out in the Prospectus of which this Application Form is part.

And I/We attach a cheque or banker's draft for the amount payable, namely	£		2

PLEASE USE BLOCK CAPITALS

Mr./Mrs./Miss or Title		Forename(s) (in full)		Surname		
Address (in full)						3
				Postcode		

I confirm that I have read the section headed "Terms and conditions of application" in Part • and the section headed "Risk Factors" in Part • of the Prospectus.

Date		Signature		4

Pin your cheque or banker's draft for the amount shown in Box 2 made payable to "•" and crossed "A/C payee only"	5

Appendix 1 – AIM Admission Document

Boxes 6 and 7 must be completed in the case of joint applicants only

Mr./Mrs./Miss or Title	6	Mr./Mrs./Miss or Title	6	Mr./Mrs./Miss or Title	6
Name(s) in full		Name(s) in full		Name(s) in full	
Address in full		Address in full		Address in full	
Postcode		Postcode		Postcode	
Signature	7	Signature	7	Signature	7

Intermediaries claiming commission should stamp the box below

Stamp of intermediary	SRO and Membership number

APPENDIX 2
TARGET PLC

AIM ADMISSION TIMETABLE –
PUBLIC OFFER WITH PLACING

\	KEY DATES
Date	Priority
[Week 1]	Front end and response to legal due diligence memorandum
[Week 2]	Initial drafts of all documentation
[Week 3]	Completion of accountants' report and legal due diligence memorandum
[Week 4]	General progress
[Week 5]	Start of verification
[Week 6]	Verification
[Week 7]	Placing proof
[Week 8]	Marketing and Impact day
[Week 9]	Payment of subscription monies
[Week 10]	Admission to AIM and commencement of dealings

A Practitioner's Guide to the Alternative Investment Market Rules

TARGET PLC

AIM ADMISSION TIMETABLE – PUBLIC OFFER WITH PLACING

Key:
ACC = Reporting accountants of Target PLC
PR = Public relations advisers
BRO = Broker and nominated adviser
SOL = Solicitors of Target PLC
COM = Target PLC

Date	Event	Responsibility
ASAP	Set provisional timetable	BRO/COM
ASAP	Directors' cards questionnaires	BRO/COM
	Finalise instruction letters (consider reporting accountants, solicitors to the company, nominated brokers, nominated advisers, PR advisers, receiving bank, registrars, surveyors and printers)	BRO/COM
	Decide on dates for organising any necessary EGM to deal with (if required): (a) group reorganisation (b) authority to allot shares and disapply pre-emption rights (c) share option requirements (d) adopt new articles	SOL
	Consult PR advisers on proposed programme of presentations and announcements	COM/BRO
	Sort out any property (including intellectual property) problems	SOL

Appendix 2 – AIM Admission Timetable

Date	Event	Responsibility
	Review what tax clearances required	SOL/ACC
	Decide on indebtedness date	ACC
	Decide on dates for drafts of working capital memorandum, report on profit forecast, memorandum on indebtedness, memorandum on financial reporting procedures	ACC
	Finalise Directors'/key employee service contracts	COM/SOL
	Sort out share options (if any)	SOL
Week 1	**Priority: Front end Admission Document and response to legal due diligence memorandum**	
Monday	Fresh timetable and list of documents	BRO/SOL
	EIS/VCT clearance sought	ACC
Tuesday	Drafting meeting (front end Admission Document)	BRO
	Draft response on legal due diligence memorandum produced	COM/SOL
Week 2	**Priority: Initial drafts of all documentation**	
Monday	Drafting meeting (back end Admission Document)	SOL/COM
Tuesday	Drafting meeting (presentation)	COM/PR
Week 3	**Priority: Completion of accountants' report and legal due diligence memorandum**	
Monday	Comments on presentation	All

Date	Event	Responsibility
Week 4	**Priority: General progress** **All parties to have submitted expense estimates**	All
	Colour and design of documents (including cover) finalised	COM/BRO
	First rehearsal of management presentation to institutions and press	PR
Week 5	**Priority: Start of verification**	
Monday	Circulate Directors' pack: (a) draft pathfinder board minutes (b) final responsibility letters (c) final powers of attorney (d) memorandum on responsibilities (e) near final placing proof	SOL
Tuesday	Verification notes/questions to be available and distributed	SOL
Friday	Progress/drafting meeting	SOL
Week 6	**Priority: Verification**	
Wednesday	Verification meeting to focus on issues raised from initial verification process	All
	Estimate of expenses finalised	COM
	Draft pathfinder press release available	PR
	Final comments on documents to be given including: (a) Admission Document	All

Appendix 2 – AIM Admission Timetable

Date	Event	Responsibility
	(b) Verification notes	
	(c) Press releases	
	Placing agreement placing letter, service agreements, restricted persons agreement finalised	SOL/BRO
Friday	All work to have been completed by this day including: (a) long and short form reports (b) working capital reports (c) indebtedness statement (d) pro forma statements (e) profit forecast (f) consent letters, comfort letters	All ACC ACC ACC ACC ACC ACC/BRO/PR/SOL
Week 7	**Priority: Placing proof**	
	10-day information notified to Exchange	BRO
	Informal pricing meeting to determine price range for discussion with institutions	COM/BRO
Tuesday	Board meeting to: (a) approve service contracts (b) approve placing proof (c) approve verification notes (d) adopt working capital statement and profit forecast (if any) (e) approve indebtedness	COM/SOL

Date	Event	Responsibility
	(f) approve placing agreement (and ancillary documents)	
	(g) approve estimate of expenses	
	(h) approve press announcement	
	(i) approve number of shares subject to placing	
	(j) approve new articles	
	(k) approve share incentive schemes	
	(l) adopt the Model dealing Code	
Wednesday	Placing proof available and sent out to institutions	BRO
	Meetings with press	COM/BRO
	Presentations to institutions	COM/BRO
Week 8	**Priority: Marketing and impact day**	
	Feedback from institutions	
Tuesday	Finalisation of price	COM/BRO
	Final proofs of Prospectus/Admission Document and other documents to be available	
	Accountants' report signed	ACC
	Board meeting to: (a) confirm issue price	COM/SOL

Appendix 2 – AIM Admission Timetable

Date	Event	Responsibility
	(b) approve all documents, including Prospectus/Admission Document, placing agreement, estimate of expenses, working capital statement, profit forecast, press announcements, new share certificates	
	(c) sign the placing agreement (to be held in escrow)	
	(d) provisionally and conditionally allot new shares	
	(e) appoint a board committee to deal with all matters connected with the offer, including the allotment of new ordinary shares	
	Directors' responsibility statements and powers of attorney signed	COM/SOL
[2 pm?]	Latest time for final price and other adjustments to the Prospectus/Admission Document to be submitted to printers	All
	Bulk print Prospectus/Admission Document	BRO
Wednesday	**IMPACT DAY – APPLICATION TO AIM**	
	Placing agreement (and other documents) released from escrow	
	Final Prospectus/Admission Document [and placing letters sent to placees]	BRO

Date	Event	Responsibility
	Prospectus/Admission Document lodged with Registrar of Companies	SOL
	Three day information submitted to Exchange: (a) Application form (b) nominated advisers' declaration (c) cheque for Exchange fee (d) six copies of Admission Document	BRO
	[Placing completed]	[BRO]
	Press release	PR
Thursday	Documents to be available for inspection for one month	SOL
Week 9	**Priority: Payment**	
Wednesday	All funds to have been received and cleared	SOL
	Board meeting to approve basis of allocation / allot shares, approve press releases and authorise despatch of documents of title	SOL/COM
Week 10	**Priority: Admission to AIM effective and commencement of dealings**	
	Announcement from Stock Exchange	BRO

Appendix 2 – AIM Admission Timetable

Date	Event	Responsibility
	Dealings commence in London	BRO
	Cash payable to vendor shareholders and company	SOL
	Definitive share certificates despatched to existing and new shareholders	

APPENDIX 3
BOARD MINUTES FOR AIM APPLICATION
PUBLIC OFFER WITH PLACING

Minutes of a meeting of the Board of Directors of the Company held at • on • at •.

Present:

Apologies:

In Attendance:

1.   Notice, quorum and declaration of interests

The Chairman confirmed that notice of the meeting had been given to all Directors entitled to receive it and noted that a quorum was present.

Pursuant to Section 317 of the Companies Act 1985 and the Articles of Association of the Company each Director declared his interest in the matters referred to below either by reason of his interest in holdings of shares in the Company and/or his being a proposed party to the placing agreement.

2.   Purpose of the meeting

The Chairman explained that the business of the meeting concerned:

(a) the proposed Offer for subscription ("the Offer") being arranged by the Company's nominated adviser, ("the Nominated Adviser") of • ordinary shares of • pence each in the Company as set out in the proposed prospectus of the Company ("the Admission Document"); and

(b) the admission to the Alternative Investment Market ("AIM") of the London Stock Exchange of all the ordinary shares of the Company issued and to be issued ("Admission").

3. **Extraordinary general meeting**

It was reported that:

(a) the resolution submitted to the extraordinary general meeting held on • had been duly passed; and
(b) by virtue of these resolutions the Directors were authorised to allot the subscription shares without any pre-emption rights applying.

4. **The Offer**

It was reported that the Nominated Adviser had informed the Company of its readiness to proceed with the Offer and that accordingly the Company was also in a position to proceed with the Offer.

5. **Production of documents**

The following documents were then produced to the meeting:

5.1 Admission Document

(a) three copies of the final draft of the Admission Document;
(b) two copies of the verification notes dated today prepared by [solicitors] by way of verification of the information contained in the Admission Document with supporting documents (together "the Verification Documents");
(c) letter from [accountants] consenting to the issue of the Admission Document with the inclusion of their reports therein.

5.2 Placing agreement

(a) an agreement (the "placing agreement") to be entered into between the Company, the Directors and the Nominated Adviser, under which the Nominated Adviser agrees (conditionally upon, *inter alia*, admission on or before • or such later date, not later than • , as the Company and the Nominated Adviser may agree) to use all reasonable endeavours to arrange for subscribers for • ordinary shares (the "Offer Shares") at the issue price;

Appendix 3 – Board Minutes for AIM Application

(b) [the placing letter to be sent by the Broker to prospective placees under the issue ("the Placing Letter")];
(c) an agreement dated • entered into between the Nominated Adviser and all shareholders [(other than the Directors)] imposing restrictions on sales of shares until publication of accounts of the Company to •.

5.3 Financial information – general

(a) copy letters appointing • ("the reporting accountants") as the reporting accountants in connection with the Admission Document and Admission procedure;
(b) two final drafts of the accountants' report on the Company.

5.4 Financial information – working capital

(a) a final draft of the letter from the reporting accountants to the Company and to the Nominated Adviser reviewing the cash forecast and reporting on the sufficiency of working capital;
(b) a copy of the working capital memorandum.

5.5 Financial information – miscellaneous

(a) a signed original of the letter from the reporting accountants to the Company and the Nominated Adviser confirming the statement as to the indebtedness of the Company as at the close of business on • contained in the Admission Document;
(b) board letter on financial reporting procedures;
(c) an estimate of the expenses of the placing.

5.6 Directors' responsibilities

(a) two memoranda prepared by [solicitors] regarding responsibilities and potential liabilities of the Directors arising in connection with the publication of the Prospectus and the continuing obligations of the Company under the London Stock Exchange's AIM Rules ("the Memoranda on Liabilities and Obligations");
(b) responsibility letter from each director addressed to the Directors of the Company and the Nominated Adviser.

5.7 Extraordinary general meeting

The resolution passed at the extraordinary general meeting held on • signed by the Chairman.

5.8   Dealing Code

(a) the Dealing Code to be adopted by the Company to ensure compliance by the Company with the AIM Rules relating to restrictions on deals;
(b) notice relating to the Dealing Code for Directors and relevant employees.

5.9   Registrars

(a) correspondence between the Company and [registrars] whereby the latter has agreed to act as the Company's registrars;
(b) a final draft of the definitive share certificate relating to the ordinary shares.

5.10   Share option scheme

The share option scheme established by the Company.

5.11   EMI option deeds

The EMI option deeds granted on • to • in respect of • ordinary shares at a price of £• per share.

5.12   [Option deeds

The options granted on • to • in respect of • ordinary shares each at a price of £• for services provided in relation to the Offer for subscription.]

5.13   Directors/staff

(a) employment agreements between the Company and • and •;
(b) letters of appointment of non-executive Directors.

5.14   Insurance

A letter dated • from •, the insurance brokers for the Company, confirming that the insurance arrangements for • are in proper order and that they are keeping under review the insurance cover presently held by them.

Appendix 3 – Board Minutes for AIM Application

6. **Admission Document and Placing Agreement**

It was explained to the Directors that a copy of the Admission Document would be filed with the Registrar of Companies. Under the Public Offers and Securities Regulations 1995, each of the Directors could be personally liable to pay compensation to persons who subscribed or subsequently purchased any of the securities on the basis of the Admission Document for loss or damage they might sustain by reason of any untrue or misleading statement included therein or omission therefrom. Unless a director had reasonable grounds for believing the same to be true he could also be criminally liable under Section 47 of the Financial Services Act 1986. The Chairman drew the attention of the Directors to the verification documents, the purpose of which was to provide a record of the steps taken to check the accuracy of the information given in the Admission Document and that the Directors and other persons referred to therein had confirmed the answers to certain questions contained therein.

The Chairman then drew the attention of the Directors to the Admission Document and, in particular, to the following sections:

(a) the indebtedness statement on the front page;
(b) the Offer statistics section on page •;
(c) the sections in Part One headed "Executive Summary" , "Risk Factors" and "the Directors";
(d) the statement of the Directors' interests in paragraphs • in Part Three;
(e) the statement in paragraph • in Part three relating to litigation;
(f) the working capital statement in paragraph • in part • ; each director having confirmed that he considered the Company to have sufficient working capital for its present requirements.

It was emphasised that the Directors were collectively and individually responsible for the accuracy of the contents of the Admission Document.

The attention of the Directors was drawn to the provisions of the Public Offers of Securities Regulations 1995 and, in particular, to Regulation 9 which has an overriding requirement that the Admission Document contains the information which, according to the particular nature of the issuer and of the securities for the admission of which application to the London Stock Exchange is being made, is necessary to enable investors to make an informed assessment of the assets and liabilities, financial position

A Practitioner's Guide to the Alternative Investment Market Rules

profit and losses and prospects of the issuer, and of the rights attaching to such securities. Their attention was drawn, in particular, to the responsibility statement on the front page of the Admission Document. Any significant new factors capable of affecting the assessment of the ordinary shares of the Company arising between the date of the Admission Document and the date on which dealings in the ordinary shares of the Company are to begin would be covered in a supplement to the Admission Document.

Each Director confirmed that he had read and was fully aware of the contents of the Admission Document and of the responsibility statement to which reference had been made and confirmed, taking into account the points to which his attention had been drawn above, that the Admission Document contained all material information and particulars with regard to the Company to comply with the requirements of the Public Offers of Securities Regulations, the AIM Rules and with all other legislation or requirements, that each was responsible for the information contained in the Admission Document and to the best of his knowledge and belief (after taking all reasonable care to ensure that such was the case) the information contained in the Admission Document was in accordance with the facts and did not omit anything likely to affect the import of such information and that he accepted responsibility accordingly.

The attention of the Directors was drawn to the fact that, as an AIM company, the Company would have continuing obligations under the AIM Rules of the London Stock Exchange. In particular, it was noted that it was a fundamental requirement that the London Stock Exchange should be informed of developments which may lead to substantial movement in the price of its securities.

The Company and each Director was bound by the Dealing Code relating to restrictions on deals which embodied the guiding principles that:

(a) Directors and relevant employees should not deal in securities of the Company on considerations of a short-term nature; and

(b) in addition to the general constraint on dealings at a time when the director or relevant employee concerned is in possession of unpublished price-sensitive information imposed by law, Directors and relevant employees would be bound not to deal in certain restricted periods prior to the publication of the interim and final results of the Company in each financial year.

Appendix 3 – Board Minutes for AIM Application

The Chairman drew attention to the warranties and indemnities to be given by the Company and the Directors in the placing agreement which was conditional, *inter alia*, on the Admission becoming effective not later than close of business on • or such later date as the Nominated Adviser and the Company may agree but in any event not later than •.

The attention of the Directors was also drawn to the restrictions on the Directors on selling shares following the Offer.

It was noted that the placing agreement would be held in escrow to be released (subject to confirmation).

It was further noted that certain employees had entered into a restricted persons' agreement with the Nominated Adviser.

7. **Resolutions**

7.1 It was resolved that:

(a) the Offer proceed at a price of •p per ordinary share ("the Offer price") and that accordingly • ordinary shares of the Company be Offered for subscription by the Company ("the subscription shares");
(b) subject to any amendments thereto as may be approved by the committee of the Board to be appointed later in the meeting, the Admission Document be and it is hereby approved and in accordance with the requirements of the Nominated Adviser one copy of the document constituting the Admission Document be signed by or on behalf of all Directors to be delivered to the Nominated Adviser and [solicitors] be instructed to deliver a copy to the Registrar of Companies for registration as a Admission Document as required by the Financial Services Act 1986 and the Nominated Adviser be requested in accordance with the AIM Rules to deliver six copies of the Admission Document at the appropriate time to the London Stock Exchange;
(c) the Verification Documents are hereby approved and two copies be signed by each of the Directors and one signed copy delivered to the Nominated Adviser;
(d) any Director be authorised to sign on the Company's behalf the application for Admission to AIM for delivery to the London Stock Exchange;

(e) the form of, and each and every term, condition and provision contained in the placing agreement be and they are hereby approved (in particular the obligation of the Company to allot new ordinary shares of the Company in accordance with the provisions thereof) and that any two Directors be and they are hereby authorised to execute the same as a deed for and on behalf of the Company; in addition, it was noted that the placing agreement and the other documents signed pursuant to the resolutions would (unless required to be dated otherwise) be dated •;

(f) signed originals of the placing agreement be delivered to [solicitors] to be held in escrow pending confirmation from the Nominated Adviser and [named Director] (failing whom any other Director) of the Company on the morning of • (or such other date as the placing agreement is dated) that the Offer should proceed, whereupon the documents would be released from escrow and arrangements made for publication and distribution of the Admission Document implemented;

(g) the estimate of expenses of the Offer produced to the meeting be and is hereby approved;

(h) the appointment of [name of registrar] as Registrars to the Company in respect of the Offer be and is hereby confirmed;

(i) all other documents produced to the meeting be and are hereby approved;

(j) the execution on behalf of the Company of all documents produced to the meeting to which the Company is a party be approved - such execution to take the form, in the case of deeds, of the execution by any two Directors and, in the case of all other documents, of the signature thereof by any Director; and

(k) the Nominated Adviser be authorised at the appropriate time to make or cause to be made an application on the Company's behalf and at the Company's expense to the London Stock Exchange for the issued ordinary shares of the Company to be admitted to AIM and that any Director be authorised on behalf of the Company to sign all documents required by the London Stock Exchange and give all such undertakings and pay all such fees and expenses as may be necessary in connection therewith and that all steps so far taken in connection with such application be approved.

Subject only to admission becoming effective on or before •, it was resolved that:

Appendix 3 – Board Minutes for AIM Application

(a) all existing share certificates be cancelled and the Registrars be authorised and instructed to issue new certificates in the form of the definitive certificate tabled to the meeting in respect of all existing issued shares in the capital of the Company;
(b) signatures of officers of the Company on certificates for the Company's shares and debentures be dispensed with;
(c) so long as the ordinary shares of the Company rank *pari passu* in all respect, they shall not bear distinguishing numbers in accordance with Section 40 of the Companies Act 1985:
  (i) the secretary be and he is hereby authorised and instructed to arrange for a seal to be prepared with the addition of the word "Securities" ("the securities seal");
  (ii) the securities seal be and is hereby adopted as the official seal of the Company for use for sealing securities issued by the Company and for sealing documents creating or evidencing securities so issued;
  (iii) the Registrars be and they are hereby authorised to use the securities seal on share loan stock and debenture certificates issued by them on the Company's behalf if appropriate, so long as the certificates concerned shall have been approved for sealing and the method or system for affixing the securities seal be controlled by the Registrars; and
  (iv) for the foregoing purposes the securities seal be placed in the custody of the Registrars to enable the Securities Seal to be affixed in accordance with the practice of the Registrars;
(d) the Dealing Code be adopted as the code of dealing to be complied with:
  (i) by the Directors of the company;
  (ii) by any employee of the Company or Director or employee of a subsidiary undertaking or parent undertaking of the Company who, because of his office or employment in the Company or subsidiary undertaking or parent undertaking, is likely to be in possession of unpublished price-sensitive information in relation to the Company or who (together with his associates, family or trusts) holds 0.5 per cent or more of the Company's shares;
(e) the notice relating to the Dealing Code be sent to all Directors and employees of the Company advising them of the dealing rules;

(f) whereas a Director or a relevant employee must not deal in any securities of the Company without advising the Chairman (or one or more other Directors designated for this purpose) in advance and receiving clearance, in the absence of the Chairman for more than two consecutive business days from the company, [another named Director] is designated to act in the place of the Chairman for the purpose of clearing dealings by other Directors and relevant employees.

8. Appointment of committee to the board

It was resolved that any two Directors be appointed to a committee of the Board:

(a) to approve any amendments to be made to the Admission Document, or to any of the documents referred to in these Minutes including, in particular, the placing agreement;
(b) to do all other things and take all other steps as might be desirable or necessary in connection with the reorganisation, the Offer and the application for Admission to AIM; and
(c) to authorise, undertake or procure all necessary arrangements for the due performance by the Company of its obligations pursuant to the placing agreement.

9. Filing, certified copies and declarations

It was resolved that:

(a) the secretary be directed to arrange for the filing with the Registrar of Companies of all necessary returns and forms;
(b) certified copies of these Minutes be supplied to the Nominated Adviser on the basis that they should be entitled to rely upon the same.

There being no further business the meeting concluded.

....
CHAIRMAN

APPENDIX 4
INDEX OF DOCUMENTS FOR AIM APPLICATION
PUBLIC OFFER WITH PLACING

Key:

ACC	=	Reporting accountants
BRO	=	Nominated broker
COM	=	AIM Co
NA	=	Nominated adviser
PR	=	Public relations advisers
SOL	=	Solicitors

1   **Preliminary documents**

    NA   List of parties

    NA   Timetable

    COM/SOL   Letters of appointment relating to solicitors, reporting accountants, nominated broker, nominated adviser, PR advisers and registrars. [Perhaps also for actuaries, surveyors receiving bank and solicitors to nominated adviser/broker.]

2   **Admission Document**

    NA/SOL   Admission Document (perhaps including pathfinder prospectus or equivalent)

3   **Placing**

    BRO/NA   Placing agreement

    BRO/NA   List of placees

    BRO/NA   Sample placing letter

    SOL   Restricted dealing agreement

4	**Verification and legal due diligence**	
	SOL/COM	Legal due diligence questionnaire (and response)
	SOL	Legal due diligence report
	SOL/NA	Verification notes (and index of supporting documents)
5	**Financial due diligence - accounts**	
	ACC	Audited accounts for last 3 years or for life of Company
6	**Financial due diligence - long form**	
	ACC	Long/short-form report
	ACC	Letter of confirmation [documents in final form]
7	**Financial due diligence - financial reporting procedures**	
	COM/ACC	Board memorandum on financial reporting procedures
	ACC	Letter from reporting accountants to be read in conjunction with memorandum on financial reporting procedures
8	**Financial due diligence - working capital**	
	COM/ACC	Working capital memorandum
	ACC	Letter on sufficiency of working capital (including copy correspondence with banks if appropriate)
9	**Financial due diligence - indebtedness statement**	
	ACC	Letter confirming statement of indebtedness

Appendix 4 – Index of Documents for AIM Application

10	**Financial information - expenses**	
	NA	Estimate of expenses of issue
11	**Directors**	
	SOL/NA	Memorandum on responsibilities and liabilities of Directors on publication of Admission Document
	SOL/NA	Memorandum on duties and responsibilities of Directors of Company
	SOL	Responsibility letters signed by Directors
	SOL	Powers of attorney signed by each director
	SOL	Directors' service agreements
	SOL	Letters of appointment for non-executive Directors
	COM/NA	Directors' questionnaires
12	**Executive share option scheme/deeds**	
	SOL/ACC	Executive share option scheme/deeds
13	**Memorandum and articles**	
	SOL	Memorandum and new articles of association
14	**Dealing Code**	
	SOL	Dealing Code
	SOL	List of Directors and relevant employees
	SOL	Notice to Directors and relevant employees

A Practitioner's Guide to the Alternative Investment Market Rules

15 **Registrars**

    SOL   Correspondence and/or agreement between the Company and Registrar of Companies

    SOL   New definitive share certificate

16 **Tax**

    [SOL/AC   S707 letter with clearance]

    ACC   Letter on taxation in Admission Document

17 **Property**

    SOL   Certificates of Title relating to premises at •

18 **Credit/loan facilities**

    COM/SOL   Facility letter/loan agreement

19 **Insurance**

    COM/SOL   Letter for insurance brokers

20 **Consent letters**

    ACC   Letter of consent

21 **Minutes**

    SOL   Board minutes approving notice of EGM to re-register as a PLC and to adopt new articles

    SOL   Notice of EGM

    SOL   Consent to short notice

    SOL   Minutes of EGM

    SOL   Resolution passed at EGM

Appendix 4 – Index of Documents for AIM Application

    SOL/NA   Board minutes approving placing proof

    SOL/NA   Board Minutes approving AIM application

    SOL   Minutes of the board allotting the shares

22 Presentations etc.

    COM   Corporate brochure/product literature

    BRO/COM   Presentations to institutions etc.

    PR/COM   Presentations to the press

    COM   Presentations to employees

    PR/COM   Questions and answers for presentations

    COM/NA   Cover for Admission Document

23 Announcements

    PR/COM   Announcement of intention to join AIM

    PR/SOL   Pathfinder announcement

    PR/SOL   Announcement of issue on impact day

    SOL/COM   Announcement to staff, customers and suppliers

    PR/NA   Announcement of issue and dealings commencing

24 Register of Companies

    SOL   Certificate of incorporation and re-registration as a PLC

    SOL   Letter to Registrar of Companies with Admission Document (if prospectus)

25 **Application to the London Stock Exchange**

COM/NA	London Stock Exchange form for application for admission signed by the Directors (72-hour document).
NA	Declaration signed by nominated adviser
BRO	Letter from nominated broker confirming its appointment
COM/NA	Letter confirming allotment has taken place
COM/NA	Fee payable to London Stock Exchange

CONTACT DIRECTORIES

DIRECTORY OF NOMINATED ADVISERS

AIB Corporate Finance Limited
85 Pembroke Road
Ballsbridge
Dublin 4
Ireland
Jarlath Quinn
00 353 1 667 0233

Altium Capital Limited
15 Portland Place
London
W1N 3AA
Stephen Georgiadis
020 7872 6300
www.apax.co.uk

Altium Capital Limited
5 Ralli Court
West Riverside
Manchester
M3 5FT
Mark Dickenson
0161 831 9133
www.apax.co.uk

ARM Corporate Finance Limited
12 Pepper Street
London
E14 9RP
Ian Fenn
Jim McGeever
020 7512 0191
www.armcf.com

Arthur Andersen
1 Surrey Street
London
WC2R 2PS
Jonathan Hinton
020 7438 3000
www.arthurandersen.com

Arthur Andersen
1 Victoria Square
Birmingham
B1 1BD
Sarah Grunewald
0121 233 2101
www.arthurandersen.com

Arthur Andersen
1 City Square
Leeds
LS1 2AL
Sarah Grunewald
0113 207 7000
www.arthurandersen.com

Beaumont Cornish Limited
Georgian House
63 Coleman Street
London
EC2R 5BB
Roland Cornish
020 7628 3396
www.beaumontcornish.co.uk

Beeson Gregory Limited
The Registry
Royal Mint Court
London
EC3N 4EY
Chris Callaway
Julia Henderson
Nicholas Rodgers
020 7488 4040
www.beeson-gregory.co.uk

Brewin Dolphin Securities Limited
48 St Vincent Street
Glasgow
G2 5TS
Elizabeth Kennedy
0141 221 7733
www.brewindolphin.co.uk

Brewin Dolphin Securities Limited
P O Box 512
National House
36 St Annes Street
Manchester
M60 2EP
Mark Brady
0161 839 4222
www.brewindolphin.co.uk

Bridgewell Corporate Finance Limited
6 Oxford Street
Nottingham
NG7 5BH
Doug Manuel
0115 941 9721
www.bridgewell.co.uk

Bridgewell Corporate Finance Limited
21 New Street
Bishopsgate
London
EC2M 4HR
Mike Sutton
020 7623 3000
www.bridgewell.co.uk

British Linen Advisers Limited
12 Melville Street
Edinburgh
EH3 7NS
William Macdonald
0131 243 8534

Brown, Shipley & Co. Limited
Founders Court
Lothbury
London
EC2R 7HE
Andrew Smith
020 7606 9833
www.brownshipley.com

Cazenove & Co.
12 Tokenhouse Yard
London
EC2R 7AN
Zofia Kwiatek
020 7588 2828
www.cazenove.com

Directory of Nominated Advisers

Charles Stanley & Company Limited
25 Luke Street
London
EC2A 4AR
Robin Dunham
020 7739 8200
www.charlesstanley.co.uk

Close Brothers Corporate Finance Limited
10 Crown Place
Clifton Street
London
EC2A 4FT
James Oliver
020 7655 3100
www.cbcf.com

Collins Stewart Limited
21 New Street
Bishopsgate
London
EC2M 4HR
Doug Manuel
020 7283 1133
www.collinsstewart.com

Corporate Synergy plc
Piercy House
7/9 Copthall Avenue
London
EC2R 7NJ
Lindsay Mair
020 7256 2576
www.corporate.uk

Credit Lyonnais Securities
Broadwalk House
5 Appold Street
London
EC2A 2DA
Simon Bennett
020 7588 4000
www.creditlyonnais.com

Credit Suisse First Boston (Europe) Limited
One Cabot Square
London
E14 4QR
Mark Seligman
020 7888 8888
www.csfb.com

Dawnay, Day Corporate Finance Limited
8-10 Grosvenor Gardens
London
SW1W 0DH
David Floyd
020 7509 4570

Deloitte & Touche
Columbia Centre
Market Street
Bracknell
Berkshire
RG12 1PA
Lionel Young
01344 454 445
www.deloitte.co.uk

Deloitte & Touche
Leda House
Station Road
Cambridge
CB1 2RN
Ann Kennedy
01223 460 222
www.deloitte.co.uk

Deloitte & Touche
Stonecutter Court
1 Stonecutter Street
London
EC4A 4TR
Lionel Young
020 7936 3000
www.deloitte.co.uk

Deutsche Bank AG London
Winchester House
1 Great Winchester Street
London
EC2N 2DB
Anthony MacWinnie
020 7545 8000
www.db.com

Ermgassen & Co Ltd
24 Lombard Street
London
EC3V 9AD
Christopher Stainforth
tel +44 (0) 20 7929 2000
fax +44 (0) 20 7929 0432
www.ermgassen.com

Ernst & Young LLP
Becket House
1 Lambeth Palace Road
London
SE1 7EU
Paul Smith
020 7928 2000
www.eyuk.com

Goodbody Corporate Finance Limited
122 Pembroke Road
Ballsbridge Park
Ballsbridge
Dublin 4
Carole Corby
00 353 1 667 0420
www.goodbody.ie

Grant Thornton
Grant Thornton House
Melton Street
Euston Square
London
NW1 2EP
Philip Secret
Gerald Beaney
020 7383 5100
www.grantthornton.co.uk

Granville Baird Limited
Mint House
77 Mansell Street
London
E1 8AF
Andrew Perkins
020 7488 1212
www.granville-plc.com

Hawkpoint Partners Limited
4 Great St Helens
London
EC3A 6HA
Jeremy Moczarski
020 7665 4500
www.hawkpoint.com

Hoare Govett Limited
250 Bishopsgate
London
EC2M 4AA
Carol Raymond
020 7678 8000
www.abnamro.com

HSBC Investment Bank plc
Vintner's Place
68 Upper Thames Street
London
EC4V 3BJ
Anthony Stewart-Jones
020 7336 9000
www.hsbc.com

IBI Corporate Finance Limited
26 Fitzwilliam Place
Dublin 2
Ireland
Gerard Heffernan
00 353 1 661 6633

ING Barings Limited
60 London Wall
London
EC2M 5TQ
Ian Douglas
020 7767 1000
www.ingbarings.com

Insinger English Trust
44 Worship Street
London
EC2A 2JT
Alexandra Cornforth
tel +44 (0) 20 7377 6161
fax +44 (0) 20 7655 6896
e-mail infocorpfin@insinger.com
www.insinger.com

Investec Bank (UK) Limited trading as Investec Henderson Crosthwaite
2 Gresham Street
London
EC2V 7QP
Simon Grafftey-Smith
020 7597 5970
www.investec.co.uk

J & E Davy
Davy House
49 Dawson Street
Dublin 2
Republic of Ireland
Tom Byrne
00 353 1 679 6363
www.davy.ie

John East & Partners Limited
Crystal Gate
28-30 Worship Street
London
EC2A 2AH
John East
020 7628 2200
www.johneastpartners.com

A Practitioner's Guide to the Alternative Investment Market Rules

Kennedy Gee Corporate Finance Ltd
19 Cavendish Square
London
W1A 2AW
Keith Lassman
020 7636 1616
www.hk.law.co.uk

Kleinwort Benson Limited trading as Dresdner Kleinwort Benson
20 Fenchurch Street
London
EC3P 3DB
Robert Murdin
020 7623 8000
www.dresdnerkb.com

KPMG Corporate Finance
8 Salisbury Square
London
EC4Y 8BB
Susan Hodge
020 7311 1000
www.kpmg.com

KPMG Corporate Finance
Saltire Court
20 Castle Terrace
Edinburgh
EH1 2EG
David McCorquodale
0131 222 2000
www.kpmg.com

KPMG Corporate Finance
2 Cornwall Street
Birmingham
B3 2DL
Stephen Halbert
0121 233 1666
www.kpmg.com

KPMG Corporate Finance
1 Forest Gate
Brighton Road
Crawley
RH11 9PT
Nick Standen
01293 652 000
www.kpmg.com

Marshall Securities Limited
Crusader House
145-157 St John Street
London
EC1V 4QJ
John Webb
020 7490 3788

Matrix Corporate Finance
9-10 Savile Row
London
W1X 1AF
Stephen Mischler
020 7439 6050
www.matrixgroup.co.uk

Directory of Nominated Advisers

Nabarro Wells & Co. Limited
Saddlers House
Gutter Lane
Cheapside
London
EC2V 6BR
John Robertson
020 7710 7400
www.nabarro-wells.co.uk

NCB Stockbrokers Limited
3 George's Dock
International Financial Services Centre
Dublin 1
Diane Hodgson
00 3531 611 5611
www.ncb.ie

NM Rothschild & Sons Limited
82 King Street
Manchester
M2 4WQ
Peter Bates
0161 827 3800
www.nmrothschild.com

Noble & Company Limited
4 th Floor
1 Frederick's Place
London
EC2R 8AB
020 7367 5600

Noble & Company Limited
76 George Street
Edinburgh
EH2 3BU
Henry Chaplin
0131 225 9677

Nomura International plc
Nomura House
1 St Martin's-le-Grand
London
EC1A 4NP
Catherine McLoughlin
020 7521 2000
www.nomura.co.uk

Numis Securities Limited
Cheapside House
138 Cheapside
London
EC2V 6LH
Henry Jenkins
020 7776 1500
www.numiscorp.com

Old Mutual Securities
2 Lambeth Hill
London
EC4V 4GG
Christopher Airey
020 7002 4600
www.omsecurities.co.uk

Old Mutual Securities
Temple Court
35 Bull Street
Birmingham
B4 6ES
Christopher Airey
0121 200 2244
www.omsecurities.co.uk

A Practitioner's Guide to the Alternative Investment Market Rules

Old Mutual Securities
1 St James Square
Manchester
M2 6DN
Kevin Wilson
0161 827 7000
www.omsecurities.co.uk

Peel, Hunt & Company Limited
62 Threadneedle Street
London
EC2R 8HP
Christopher Holdsworth-Hunt
Adam Hart
020 7418 8900
www.peelhunt.com

PricewaterhouseCoopers
1 London Bridge
London
SE1 9QL
Peter Clokey
020 7939 3000
www.pwcglobal.com

PricewaterhouseCoopers
Plumtree Court
London
EC4A 4HT
William Morgan
Mark Speller
020 7582 5000
www.pwcglobal.com

Rathbone Neilson Cobbold Limited
Port of Liverpool Building
Pier Head
Liverpool
L3 1NW
Mike Sawbridge
0151 236 6666
www.rathbones.com

Robert Fleming & Co. Limited
25 Copthall Avenue
London
EC2R 7DR
Jeremy Kean
020 7638 5858
www.flemings.com

Rowan Dartington & Co. Limited
7th Floor
The Colston Centre
Bristol
BS1 4XE
John Wakefield
0117 933 0020
www.rowan-dartington.co.uk

Salomon Brothers UK Equity Limited
111 Buckingham Palace Road
London
SW1W 0SB
James Anderson
020 7721 2000

Seymour Pierce Limited
2nd Floor
29/30 Cornhill
London
EC3V 3NF
Richard Feigen
020 7648 8700
www.seymourpierce.com

SG Securities (London) Limited
Exchange House
Primrose Street
London
EC2A 2DD
David Mordaunt
020 7638 9000
www.socgen.com

Shore Capital & Corporate Limited
Bond Street House
14 Clifford Street
London
W1X 1RE
Graham Shore
020 7734 7293
www.shorecap.co.uk

Smith & Williamson
No1 Riding House Street
London
W1A 3AS
Dr A. Basirov
020 7637 5377
www.smith.williamson.co.uk

Société Générale trading as SG Hambros
SG House
41 Tower Hill
London
EC3N 4SG
Roger Bawcutt
020 7676 6000
www.socgen.co.uk

Solomon Hare Corporate Finance
Oakfield House
Oakfield Grove
Clifton
Bristol
BS8 2BN
Stephen Toole
0117 933 3344
www.solomonhare.co.uk

Strand Partners Limited
110 Park Street
London
W1Y 3RB
Richard Fenhalls
020 7409 3494

Teather & Greenwood Limited
Beaufort House
15 St. Botolph Street
London
EC3A 7QR
Jeremy Delmar-Morgan
020 7426 9000
www.teathers.com

UBS Warburg
1 Finsbury Avenue
London
EC2M 2PP
Michael Lacey-Solymar
020 7567 8000
www.wdr.com

WestLB Panmure Limited
Woolgate Exchange
25 Basinghall Street
London
EC2V 5HA
Richard Potts
020 7020 4000
www.westlbpanmure.com

Williams de Broë Plc
P O Box 515
6 Broadgate
London
EC2M 2RP
Tim Worlledge
020 7588 7511

Williams de Broë Plc
1 Waterloo Street
Birmingham
B2 5PG
Ian R Stanway
0121 609 0050

Williams de Broë Plc
4 Park Place
Leeds
LS1 2RU
Joanne Lake
0113 243 1619

For further information, call the AIM Team on 020 7797 4404

DIRECTORY OF COMPANIES TRADING ON AIM

7 Group plc

10 Group plc

A

Aberdeen Football Club plc

Abinger Investments plc

Access Plus plc

Acquisitor plc

Actif Group plc

ActionLeisure plc

Adaptive Venture Managers plc

AdVal Group plc

Advance Capital Invest plc

Advanced Technology (UK) plc

Advanced Visual Communications plc

ADVFN.Com plc

Aero Inventory plc

African Gold plc

Airow plc

Albemarle & Bond Holdings plc

Alexanders Holdings plc

Alibi Communications plc

Ambient plc

Amco Corporation plc

Andaman Resources plc

Anglo Siberian Oil Company plc

Anglo-Welsh Group plc

Antonov plc

AorTech International plc

Aquarius Group plc

Aquarius Platinum Limited

Arko Energy Holdings plc

Arlington Group plc

Artisan (UK) plc

Ashquay Group plc

ASK Central plc

Aspinalls Online plc

ATA Group plc

Athelney Trust plc

Atlantic Caspian Resources plc

Atlantic Global plc
Aulron Energy Ltd
Auto Indemnity Group plc
auxinet plc
Axiomlab Plc

B

Bakery Services plc
Bank Restaurant Group plc
Baron Corporation plc
Basepoint plc
Beaufort Group plc
Belgravium Technologies plc
Betinternet.com plc
Bidtimes plc
Big Yellow Group plc
Bikenet plc
Billam plc
Bilston & Battersea Enamels plc
Biofocus plc
BioLife Ventures plc
Birchin International plc
Birmingham City plc
Bits Corp plc

Bizspace plc
Bizzbuild.com plc
Black Rock Oil & Gas plc
Blavod Black Vodka plc
Blazepoint Group plc
Blooms of Bressingham Holdings plc
Bogod Group plc
Bond International Software plc
Bowness Leisure plc
Braindock.com, Inc
Brainspark plc
Brancote Holdings plc
Bristol & West Investments plc
British Bloodstock Agency plc (The)
BSOFTB plc
Buckland Investments plc
Bulgin plc
Burnden Leisure plc
Buyers Guide Plc
BV Group Plc

C

C & B Publishing plc

Directory of Companies Trading on AIM

C.A. Coutts Holdings plc

Caledonian Trust plc

Cambridge Mineral Resources plc

Capcon Holdings plc

CapitalTech plc

Carbo plc

Carlisle Holdings Limited

Cassidy Brothers plc

Cater Barnard plc

Celltalk Group (The) plc

Channel Health Plc

channelfly plc

Charlton Athletic plc

Charterhouse Communications plc

Charteris plc

Chelford Group plc

Chelsea Village plc

Chorion plc

Civilian Content plc

Claims People Group (The) plc

Clan Homes plc

Clarity Commerce Solutions plc

Clipper Ventures plc

Clipserver plc

Clover Corporation Limited

Cluff Mining plc

CMS Webview Plc

Coliseum Group plc

comeleon plc

Comland Commercial plc

Communitie.com Limited

Compass Software Group Plc

Comprehensive Business Services plc

ComProp Limited

ComputerLand UK plc

Concurrent Technologies plc

Conder Environmental plc

Conister Trust plc

Connaught plc

Conroy Diamonds and Gold plc

Constellation Corporation plc

Contemporary Enterprises plc

ControlP plc

Convergence Holdings plc

Cook (D.C.) Holdings plc
Corac Group plc
Corporate Synergy Holdings plc
Corum plc
Corvus Capital Inc
Countyweb.com plc
CPL Resources plc
CRC Group plc
Cresco International plc
CSS Stellar plc
Cube8 Group plc
CW Residential plc
CyberChina Holdings plc
Cyberes plc
CybIT Holdings plc
Cytomyx Holdings plc

D

Deep-Sea Leisure plc
Delcam plc
Desire Petroleum plc
Digital Animations Group plc
Digital Classics plc
Digital Sport plc

Dimension Resources Limited
Dinkie Heel plc
Direct Message plc
Dobbies Garden Centres plc
Domino's Pizza UK & IRL plc
Downtex plc
Dynamic Commercial Finance plc

E

Eagle Eye Telematics plc
Earthport plc
Easier plc
E-Capital Investments plc
e-district.net plc
Einstein Group plc
Electric Word plc
Electronic Retailing Systems International, inc
Elite Strategies plc
EMDEXTRADE Plc
emondo.com plc
Empire Interactive Plc
Enterprise plc
EnterpriseAsia.com plc

Directory of Companies Trading on AIM

Envesta plc

Environmental Polymers Group plc

Epic Group plc

e-primefinancial plc

Equator Group plc

e-quisitor plc

Era Group plc

Eurasia Mining plc

Eurocity Properties plc

Eurolink Managed Services plc

European Diamonds plc

European Telecom plc

EuroTelecom Communications Inc

Eurovestech plc

Evolution Group (The) plc

e-xentric plc

F

Fairplace Consulting plc

Fayrewood plc

FfastFill plc

Fieldens plc

Finelot plc

Firestone Diamonds plc

First Property Online plc

First Quantum Minerals Ltd

Fish plc

Fiske plc

Flomerics Group plc

Focus Solutions Group plc

Forbidden Technologies plc

Forever Broadcasting plc

Formscan plc

Fountains plc

French plc

FTV Group plc

Fulcrum Pharma plc

Fundamental-e Investments plc

Fusion Oil & Gas plc

Future Integrated Telephony plc

Future Internet Technologies plc

G

G.R. (Holdings) plc

Galahad Capital plc

gameplay plc

Gaming Internet plc

GB Railways Group plc
Genus plc
Georgica plc
Getmapping.com plc
Giardino Group plc
Globalnet Financial.com Inc
Glow Communications plc
Goal plc
Gold Mines of Sardinia Limited
Golden Prospect plc
Gooch & Housego plc
Greenchip Investments plc
Griffin Mining Limited
Grosvenor Land Holdings plc
GTL Resources plc
Guiton Group Limited
GW Pharmaceuticals plc

H

Hacas Group plc
Halladale Group plc
Hansard Group plc
Harrier Group plc
Harrogate Group plc
Hartest Holdings plc
Hartford Group plc
Hat Pin plc
Hay (Norman) plc
Headway plc
Heath (Samuel) & Sons plc
Heavitree Brewery plc (The)
hemscott.NET Group plc
Hereward Ventures plc
Hidefield plc
Highams Systems Services Group plc
Highland Timber plc
Honeycombe Leisure plc
Honeysuckle Group plc
Host Europe PLC
Hunters Leisure plc
Hurlingham PLC
Hydro-Dynamic Products plc

I

I Feel Good (Holdings) plc
I^{2}S plc
IBNet plc

Directory of Companies Trading on AIM

ID Data plc
Ideal Shopping Direct plc
IDN Telecom plc
i-documentsystems Group plc
IFTE plc
Illuminator plc
Impax Group plc
IMS MAXIMS plc
Imprint Search and Selection plc
Inflexion plc
Ingenta plc
Innobox plc
Innovision Research & Technology plc
InTechnology plc
Integrated Asset Management plc
Intelligent Environments Group plc
Intelliplus Group plc
Interactivity Group plc
Intercede Group plc
Inter Link Foods plc
Inter-Alliance Group plc

Interclubnet Plc
Interior Services Group plc
Intermediate Equity plc
International Greetings plc
Internet Business Group plc
Internet Direct plc
Internet Incubator plc
Internet Music and Media plc
Interregnum plc
Inventive Leisure plc
iomart Group plc
IQ-Ludorum Plc
i-spire plc
IT IS Holdings Plc

J

J2C plc
JAB Holdings Limited
James R. Knowles (Holdings) plc
Jamies Bars plc
Jarvis Porter Group plc
Jennings Brothers plc
Jetcam International Holdings Limited

Jobs.co.uk plc

John Lewis of Hungerford plc

Jumbo International plc

Just Group plc

K

K3 Business Technology Group plc

Kazoo3D plc

Keryx Biopharmaceuticals Inc

Keyworld Investments plc

Kingsbridge Holdings Plc

Knowledge Technology Solutions plc

L

Lady In Leisure Group plc

Landround plc

Lawrence plc

Legendary Investments plc

Lepco plc

LiDCO Group Plc

Lighthouse Group plc

Linton Park plc

Lionheart plc

Loades plc

Lok'n Store Group plc

Lombard Medical plc

London Securities plc

London Town plc

Longbridge International plc

Longmead Group plc

Lonrho Africa plc

M

Maclellan Group plc

Madisons Coffee plc

Maelor plc

Magnum Power plc

Majestic Wine plc

Mano River Resources Inc.

Market Age (The) Plc

Martin Shelton Group plc

Matrix Healthcare plc

Maverick Entertainment Group plc

Meanfiddler.com plc

Mears Group plc

Medi@Invest plc

Media Content plc

Directory of Companies Trading on AIM

Media Square plc
Mediwatch plc
Medical House (The) plc
Medical Marketing International Group plc
Megalomedia plc
Mercury Recycling Group plc
Metnor Group plc
Metrodome Group plc
Mettoni Group plc
Mezzanine Group plc
Millfield Group plc
Minco plc
Minorplanet Systems plc
Mission Testing plc
Mobilefuture plc
Mondas plc
MoneyGuru Group plc
Money Channel plc (The)
Monotub Industries plc
MotionPoster plc
Mottram Holdings plc
Mountcashel plc

Mulberry Group plc
Murchison United NL
Murray Financial Corporation plc
MV Sports Group plc
Myratech.net plc

N

Names.co Internet plc
NanoUniverse plc
NBA Quantum plc
Net b2b2 plc
Netcall plc
Netcentric Systems plc
netvest.com plc
Netwindfall plc
New Media Industries plc
Newmark Technology Group plc
NewMedia SPARK plc
Newsplayer Group plc
NFF Plc
Ninth Floor (The) plc
NMT Group plc
Non-League Media plc

Northacre plc
Northern Petroleum plc
Nottingham Forest plc
NRX Global Corp
Numis Corporation plc
NWF Group plc

O

Oasis Healthcare plc
Offshore Telecom plc
Offshore Tool & Energy Corporation
Old Monk Company plc (The)
OMG plc
OneClickHR plc
ONESATURDAY Plc
On-Line plc
Online Sports & Leisure plc
Online Travel Corporation plc
Optoplast plc
Orchard Furniture plc
Osborne & Little plc
Osprey Communications plc
Overnet Data plc

Oxus Mining plc
Oystertec plc

P

Palmaris Capital plc
Pan Andean Resources plc
Paradigm Media Investments plc
Pathfinder Properties plc
Patientline plc
PC Medics Group plc
Peel Holdings plc
Peel Hotels plc
Pennant International Group plc
Personal Group Holdings plc
Perthshire Leisure plc
Petra Diamonds Limited
Petra Multimedia plc
Petrel Resources plc
Photo-Scan plc
Pilat Technologies International Limited
PipeHawk plc
Po Na Na Group plc
podia group plc

Directory of Companies Trading on AIM

Poptones Group Plc

Portman Limited

Potential Finance Group Plc

Premier Direct Group plc

Premier Management Holdings plc

PremiSys Technologies plc

Preston North End plc

PrimeEnt plc

PrintPotato.com plc

Private & Commercial Finance Group plc

Proactive Sports Group plc

Probus Estates plc

Profile Media Group plc

Propan Homes plc

Property Internet plc

Protec PLC

Proteome Sciences plc

Pubs 'n' Bars plc

Pure Entertainment Games plc

Pursuit Dynamics plc

Q

Quadranet plc

R

Radio First plc

Raft International plc

Ramco Energy plc

Range Cooker Company Plc (The)

Rapid Technology Group plc

Razorback Vehicles Corporation Limited

RDL Group plc

Real Affinity plc

Reflec plc

ReGen Therapeutics plc

ReNeuron Holdings plc

Retail Stores plc

RexOnline plc

Riceman Insurance Investments plc

RMR plc

Robotic Technology Systems plc

RTS Networks Group plc

S

Safestore plc

Samedaybooks.co.uk plc

A Practitioner's Guide to the Alternative Investment Market Rules

Savoy Asset Management plc
SBS Group plc
Science Systems plc
Screen plc
Send Group plc
Sefton Resources Inc.
Selector Limited
Seymour Pierce Group plc
Shalibane plc
Sherry FitzGerald plc
Sibir Energy plc
Sigma Technology Group plc
Silentpoint plc
Sira Business Services plc
SMF Technologies plc
Sodra Petroleum AB
Software for Sport Plc
Solid State Supplies plc
Solitaire Group plc
Sopheon plc
Soundtracs plc
Southern Vectis plc
Sportingbet.com (UK) plc

Sports Resource Group plc
Sportscard Group plc
Springboard plc
SpringHealth Leisure plc
Staffing Ventures plc
StartIT.com plc
Startup Station plc
Stenoak Associated Services plc
Stilo International Plc
Stockcube plc
Stratus Holdings plc
Stream Group plc
Streetnames plc
Surface Technology Systems plc
Surgical Innovations Group plc
Sutton Harbour Holdings plc
Synigence plc
Systems Integrated Research plc
Systems International Group plc
Systems Union Group plc

T

Tandem Group plc
Transcomm plc

Directory of Companies Trading on AIM

TCT International plc

tecc-IS PLC

Technology and Internet Property Services plc

Tenon Group plc

Tepnel Life Sciences plc

Tera Group plc

Tertiary Minerals plc

thebiz.com plc

themutual.net plc

Theo Fennell plc

Thomas Potts plc

Thomson Intermedia plc

ThreeW.net plc

Tiger Resource Finance plc

Tikit Group plc

Time2Learn plc

Tolent plc

Tolmount plc

Tom Hoskins plc

Topnotch Health Clubs plc

Tornado Group plc

Totalise plc

Totally plc

Transacsys plc

Transcomm plc

TransEDA plc

Transense Technologies plc

Transport Systems plc

TranXenoGen Inc

Tribal Group plc

Trinity Care plc

U

UA Group plc

UBC Media Group plc

Ultimate Leisure Group plc

Underwriting & Subscription plc

Union plc

Unite Group plc

United Industries plc

Univent plc

Universe Group plc

V

Vema N.V.

Veos plc

VFG plc

VI Group plc
VIANET Group plc
Victory Corporation plc
Viking Internet plc
Virotec International Limited
Virtual Internet plc
virt-x plc
Voss Net plc

W

W. H. Ireland Group plc
Wap Integrators Plc
Warthog plc
Water Hall Group plc
Wealth Management Software plc
Weatherly International plc
Web Shareshop (Holdings) plc
Web-angel plc
Weeks Group plc (The)
West 175 Media Group Inc.
West Bromwich Albion plc
Western Selection plc
Westmount Energy Limited

Westside Acquisitions plc
WILink.com plc
William Nash plc
Willington plc
Winchester Entertainment plc
World Careers Network plc
World Life Sciences plc
World Travel Holdings plc
Wyatt Group plc
Wynnstay Properties plc

X

Xpertise Group plc
XS Leisure plc
Xworks plc

Y

Yeoman Group plc

Z

Zipcom plc
Zoa Corporation plc
Zytronic plc

For further information, call the AIM Team on 020 7797 4404

INDEX

NB: All references are to chapter number followed by paragraph number, e.g. 4.9.1 refers to Chapter 4, paragraph 9.1

admission document 1.5, 4.2
   authorised persons 2.8
   contents of 2.5, 4.2
   directors' histories 4.9.1
   directors' responsibilities 4.7.2, 4.7.3, 4.9.2, 4.9.3
   evidence and confirmation 4.7.3
   further admission documents 2.6, 5.6
   indebtedness statement 4.8.5
   mis-statements 2.8
   profit forecasts 4.8.4
   publication of 2.4, 4.2
   regulation of 2.8
   requirement for 2.1, 4.2
   taxation 4.10
   verification notes 4.7.1, 4.7.4
   working capital statement 4.8.3
   see also **admission to AIM**; **prospectuses**
admission fees 3.2.1, 5.8.7
admission to AIM 1.1
   application to Stock Exchange 4.12
   board meetings 4.4.3-4.4.5
   charges 4.12.3
   company requirements 3.2, 3.2.1, 4.1
   dealing codes 4.9.7
   declaration by nominated adviser 3.4.7, 4.12.4
   directors
      power of attorney 4.9.4
   EGMs 4.4.2
   financial due diligence 4.8
   index of documents 4.3.1
   insurance confirmation 4.11
   issuing of a dealing notice 4.12.5
   legal due diligence 4.3.5
   letter from nominated broker 4.12.4
   letters of appointment 4.3.4
   list of parties 4.3.2
   overseas companies 3.2.3
   placing agreements 4.6
   public relations issues 4.5
   reverse takeovers 5.5.4
   share structure 3.2.3
   structure of companies 3.2.3, 4.4.1
   timetable 4.3.3
   see also **admission document**
'agency crosses' 6.7
Alternative Investment Market (AIM) 1.1
   companies
      disciplinary action against 3.6.3, 3.6.5
      eligibility criteria 5.8
      provision of information to Stock Exchange 3.5.1, 3.5.2
      publishing information 3.5.1
      sources of information on 6.10
   regulation of 2.1
   rules 1.6, 2.1, 3.1,7.6
      appeals 3.6.6
      breach of 3.6.3
      contents 3.1
   rule 19 7.1
      breach of 7.9
   size of 1.7
   sources of information on 1.7
annual accounts
   publication of 5.4.1
annual fees 3.2.1, 5.8.7
audit committees 8.1, 8.6

Cadbury Code 8.1
CAO *see* **Company Announcements Office**
City Code on Takeovers and Mergers 5.7
classifiable transactions 5.5
    aggregation of transactions 5.5.5
    class tests 5.5, 5.5.1
    examples of 5.5
    related party transactions 5.5.3
    reverse takeovers 5.5.4
    substantial transactions 5.5.2
close periods
    definition of 3.3.4, 7.4
Companies Act 1985 2.2.3
Company Announcements Office (CAO)
    disclosure requirements *see* **disclosure requirements**
connected persons
    dealings 7.3, 7.8
corporate governance 8.1, 8.2, 8.5, 8.6
    Combined Code of best practice 8.4
    voting 8.7
CREST 3.2.1, 6.8

dealing codes 4.9.7, 6.9.1.5
dealing notices
    issuing of 4.12.5
directors
    accountability *see* **corporate governance**
    dealings 7.3
    disclosure requirements 3.3.3, 3.3.6, 5.3.5, 7.7
    employees of 7.2, 7.8
    interests, changes in 5.3.4
    power of attorney 4.9.4
    questionnaires 4.9.1
    re-election of 8.6
    remuneration 8.5
    responsibilities 3.3.5, 4.7.2, 4.7.3, 4.9.2, 4.9.3, 5.8.8
    role of 3.3.1, 8.6
    seeking advice from nominated advisers 3.3.7

service contracts 3.3.1, 4.9.5
share dealing 3.3.4, 5.8.4, 6.9.1.5, 6.9.2.1
training 8.6
warranties 4.6.3-4.6.5
disclosure requirements 5.2, 5.3.1, 5.3.9
    board changes 5.3.5
    dealing announcements 6.9.2
    directors 3.3.3, 3.3.6, 5.3.5
    directors' interests 5.3.4
    dividend payments 5.3.8
    nominated advisers 3.4.1, 5.3.6
    nominated brokers 5.3.6
    number of shares in issue 5.3.7
    price-sensitive information 5.3.1, 7.5
    share price movements 5.3.1
    shareholders 5.3.3
    trading performance and forecasts 5.3.2
    see also **classifiable transactions; financial reporting**
disposal of shares
    restrictions on 3.3.2, 4.6.6
dividend payments 5.3.8

EC Prospectus Directive 2.2.1
EGMs 4.4.2
eligibility criteria 5.8
employees 7.2
EMI schemes 4.9.6
Enterprise Management Incentives (EMI) schemes 4.9.6
expenses of issue 4.8.6
extraordinary general meetings (EGMs) 4.4.2

financial due diligence 4.8
    board memorandum on financial reporting procedures 4.8.2
    forms of reports 4.8.1
    see also **financial reporting**
financial promotions 2.2.5, 4.5
    see also **investment advertisements**
financial reporting 3.2.1, 5.4
    see also **financial due diligence**

Index

firm continuous two-way prices 6.4.2
firm exposure orders 6.4.1
free market capital (FMC) 6.5

half-yearly reports *see* interim reports
Hampel Committee 8.1, 8.5, 8.6, 8.7
'hit order price' 6.4.1

IMAS 6.9.3
indebtedness statements 4.8.5
indicative exposure orders 6.4.1
'inside information'
   definition of 6.9.1.1
insider dealing
   civil liability 6.9.1.3
   criminal liability 6.9.1.1
   defences to 6.9.1.1, 6.9.1.2
   FSA code 6.9.1.4
   market makers 6.9.1.2
insurance 4.11
integrated monitoring and surveillance system (IMAS) 6.9.3
interim reports
   publication of 5.4.2
investment advertisements 2.2.4
   see also financial promotions
investor protection 3.6.2
issue board meetings 4.4.5

legal due diligence 4.3.5
letters of appointment 4.3.4
liquidity 6.5, 6.9.3

'market abuse' 2.7.1, 6.9.1.4
market makers 3.2.1, 6.2, 6.3, 6.4.2
   insider dealing 6.9.1.2
   substantial interests 6.9.2.2
matched bargain basis 6.4.1

nominated advisers
   admission fees 5.8.7
   annual fees 3.4.4.8, 5.8.7
   appeals 3.4.5.5
   application process 3.4.3.5
   conflicts of interest 3.4.4.2, 3.4.6
   declarations 3.4.7, 4.12.4
   disciplinary action 3.4.5.3, 3.6.4, 3.6.5
   disclosure requirements 3.4.1, 5.3.6
   eligibility criteria 1.2, 3.4.1, 3.4.2, 3.4.3
   fees charged by 3.4.6
   independence 3.4.4.1
   notice periods 3.4.6, 5.8.2
   ongoing experience of corporate finance 3.4.4.6
   operating procedures 3.4.4.4
   performance reviews 1.2, 3.4.5.1
   preventing from acting as 3.4.5.4
   provision of information to Stock Exchange 3.4.8
   qualified executives 3.4.4.9, 3.4.5.2
   records, maintenance of 3.4.4.7
   register of 1.2
   rejection of 3.4.3.4
   requirement for 3.4.1, 3.6.1
   responsibilities 3.4.4.3, 3.4.8
   role of 1.1, 1.2, 1.4, 3.1, 3.3.7, 3.4.1, 3.4.6
   screening companies 1.3, 3.2.2
   staffing requirements 3.4.4.5
   terms of engagement 3.4.6
nominated brokers
   'agency crosses' 6.7
   disclosure requirements 5.3.6
   eligibility criteria 3.2.1
   information to market makers 6.4.2
   letters of appointment 4.12.4
   maintaining after-market 6.6
   need for 5.8.3
   notice periods 3.6.1
   pricing new issues 6.6
   publicising information amongst client-base 6.6
   relations with investors 6.7
   role of 3.2.1, 6.4, 6.4.1
non-executive directors
   liability 4.6.4

A Practitioner's Guide to the Alternative Investment Market Rules

overseas companies 3.2.3

pathfinder board meetings 4.4.3
Paying for Performance : The New Framework for Executive Remuneration 8.5
placing agreements
    conditionality of obligations of nominated advisers 4.6.1
    obligations of nominated brokers 4.6.2
    restrictions on disposals of shares 4.6.6
    warranties 4.6.3-4.6.5
placing proof 4.4.3
power of attorney 4.9.4
preliminary statements of annual results 5.4.1
price-sensitive information
    definition of 3.3.4
    disclosure requirements 5.3.1
    insider dealing 6.9.1.1
profit forecasts 4.8.4, 5.4.2
    material difference to trading performance 5.3.2
prospectuses
    civil liability 2.7.2
    contents 2.5
    criminal liability 2.7.1
    filing of 2.4
    legislation 2.2, 2.3
    publication of 2.4
        exemptions 2.3.4
    supplementary copies 2.6
    see also admission document
Public Offers of Securities Amendment Regulations 1999 2.2.2
    scope of 2.3
Public Offers of Securities Regulations 1995 2.2.2
public relations agencies
    role of 4.5
publishing of transactions 6.8

re-election of directors 8.6
regulation of AIM 2.1

related party transactions 5.5.3
remuneration committees 8.5, 8.6
reporting transactions 6.8
residual settlement 6.8
restricted persons agreement 4.6.6
reverse takeovers 5.5.4, 5.6
Rule 19
    breach of 7.9
    definition 7.1
    exemptions 7.6
    unpublished price sensitive information 7.5

SARs 6.9.2.3
SEAQ system 6.2
SEATS PLUS trading system 3.2.1, 6.2
    information requirements 6.3
securities to be admitted 3.2.1, 5.8.6
service contracts
    directors 4.9.5
settlement arrangements 3.2.1, 5.8.3, 6.8
share for share exchange agreements 4.4.1
share option schemes 3.2.4, 4.9.6
share price movements
    monitoring of 5.3.1, 6.9.3
share prices
    status of 6.4.2
shareholders
    changes in 5.3.3
    obtaining information about 5.3.3
    substantial transactions 5.5.2
    voting 8.7
statutory framework 2.1
Substantial Acquisition Rules (SARs) 6.9.2.3
substantial interests
    disclosure requirements 6.9.2.2
substantial transactions 5.5.2
suspending trading in shares 3.4.1, 3.6.1, 3.6.2, 5.3.6, 5.5.4

takeovers 5.7
taxation 4.10
trade reports 6.8

Index

training
    directors 8.6
transferability of shares 3.2.1, 5.8.5

verification notes 4.7.1, 4.9.3
    confidentiality 4.7.4
    scope of 4.7.4
voting
    shareholders 8.7

warranties 3.4.6, 4.6.3
    limitations on 4.6.4
    time limits 4.6.5
working capital statements 4.8.3